D0504260

"IT'S ONLY
BANTER"

"IT'S ONLY BANTER"

THE AUTOBIOGRAPHY OF
LEROY ROSENIOR

LEROY ROSENIOR WITH LEO MOYNIHAN

FOREWORD BY ANDREW COLE

First published by Pitch Publishing, 2017

Pitch Publishing
A2 Yeoman Gate
Yeoman Way
Worthing
Sussex
BN13 3QZ

www.pitchpublishing.co.uk
info@pitchpublishing.co.uk

ISBN 978-1-78531-208-3

Typesetting and origination by Pitch Publishing

Printed and bound in Great Britain by TJ International

Contents

Dedication

For my late father, Willie Rosenior.
I hope I make you proud.

Acknowledgements

EVER since I can remember, my life has revolved around family so I'd like to start by thanking all of my sisters, Lauren, Lynda, Lorna, and Lena, and my wonderful mum Gladys, for all their love and support, and also my brothers-in-law, 'H', Jimmy and Sam. At home, thank you to my beautiful partner Luci and our gorgeous kids, Millie, Ethan, and Max. Thank you to my first wife, Karen and our two grown up boys, Liam and Daron, my daughter-in-law Erika and my grandkids, Leia, Issa, Ava and Nadia; you all make me the man I am…which I hope is a good thing!

At Pitch Publishing a big thank you to Paul and Jane for their support, Dean Rockett, Graham Hales, Margaret Murray, Duncan Olner, Derek Hammond and to Gareth Davis for his editing skills. Also a big thank you to Darren Lewis and Justyn Barnes for their valuable work at the beginning of this process.

Many people have lent their voices to this book and I'd like to thank each and every one of them for their time and memories.

And not forgetting Andrew Cole for his generous foreword.

Last but not least, thank you Leo Moynihan. Leo was introduced to me at a time when I had given up all hope of getting this book written. I really wanted somebody to get this story over sympathetically and without bitterness and for me, that is what Leo has done and I'll never be able to thank him enough.

Leroy Rosenior, December 2016

Foreword

I HAD a very West Indian upbringing and was always taught to respect my elders. Little surprise then that when we both arrived in Bristol, I was immediately courteous to Leroy Rosenior!

I left London a very determined young man, eager to prove myself in the game and desperate to prove the people who had decided I wasn't good enough to break into Arsenal's first team, very wrong.

Even then I knew I could play top-flight football so when the opportunity came for me to go to Bristol City I didn't hesitate, even if it meant dropping a division. Youngsters today might sulk, or stay put, satisfied with the big money they might have got at an early age, but I was so determined and as it turned out, it was the perfect place for me to go. I had other offers that nearly came off when I was on loan at City, but when the club offered to make my move permanent, I didn't flinch. 'Come on,' I said to myself. 'Let's crack on.'

Leroy's presence proved a big factor in how much I enjoyed my time and prospered at Bristol City. The two of us shared a hotel which made my move easier because I did miss the life I had built in London and my girlfriend down there. I was still a teenager, so those things can affect you, but with Leroy – a senior pro, and more importantly a very friendly guy – around to help me, I hit the ground running on the pitch and got on with kick-starting my career.

I knew of Leroy from his days at West Ham. He had done well there and what I recall was having an idea of just how good in the air he was. This though was before the days of mass football coverage so I'd be lying if I said I knew a lot about his game, and how he liked to play. He didn't stop telling me about his bad knee though, so I knew that might hinder him a bit but soon, as we began to train together and play, I could see this was a guy who could help me score some goals.

When I was young, I loved listening to senior pros. I had joined Arsenal because the likes of Tony Adams, Michael Thomas and David Rocastle had sat me down and talked to me about the game and the club. So, when it didn't work out there, I went to Bristol and that's what I did again. I listened.

There were some great senior pros at Ashton Gate and I learnt from each and every one of them: Wayne Allison, Dariusz Dziekanowski, Terry Connor and of course, Leroy. Not many young strikers are fortunate enough to have that amount of experience and attacking talent to tap into and I made sure I listened and took things from them all.

Leroy was especially forthcoming with advice. With his career coming to an end you could tell the idea of coaching excited him and he was brilliant at communicating with players. He had my respect immediately (not only because of his age!) and I knew the advice he was giving me was going to prove valuable.

It worked well for me. City spent a lot of money after I'd scored goals on loan with them, and while some senior pros there might have raised an eyebrow at the club spending their entire budget (£500,000 on a 21-year-old was a lot for a club like City back then) on one young striker, I always had the support of Leroy and his continued assistance made my life and my football that much easier.

I never felt under pressure, it was like being in the youth team at Arsenal. I'm not saying the quality wasn't good, it was and it was tough, but I just went out and played. With those goals catching the eye, Kevin Keegan came looking at me, and a big-money move to an up-and-coming Newcastle United was on the table.

I actually went to Leroy, asking if he knew any agents. He put me on to one and without naming any names, Leroy's help cost me about £30,000! I hope this book sells well, Leroy, because I might be asking for some of that back!

My connection with the Roseniors continued in the latter part of my career when, at Fulham, I played with Leroy's son Liam. Liam was a great player and a chip off the old block in terms of his enthusiasm, work ethic, talent and like me with his old man, he was keen to learn. Like his dad, he also always had an opinion and I can see him going far into management if that's the path he chooses. I hope he does.

The game needs more black coaches and managers. I speak to lots of young black footballers who blatantly rule out the idea of coaching because they don't see it as a viable option. Hopefully the likes of Liam can prove them wrong.

I was a young, football-mad kid in the 1980s and watching football, Cyrille Regis was my hero. Like so many guys of my generation, I owe a debt of gratitude to guys like him and Leroy who put up with so much abuse both on and off the pitch, making it easier for my generation to follow our dreams.

Don't get me wrong, I would never have let some racist bigot hinder the ambitions I had, but books like Leroy's are so important in highlighting what players went through and pointing out that while racism as it was in his day has been fought against and largely eradicated, the fight continues.

Andrew Cole, 2016

Prologue

The First Time

A YOUNG man with something to prove. That's what I am. Yes, I've made it, kind of. I'm a professional footballer. A teenager living his dream. A young man who wakes up, goes to work, plays football (the game I have always loved) and for my trouble, I get paid. Each weekend I run out in front of thousands of fans and do my best to score goals and win matches. When I do my job, those fans sing my name. Me, young Leroy Rosenior from Clapham. *Leroy, Leroy, Leroy.*

When I leave the ground they stop and ask me for my autograph. This is the early 1980s and whilst so many young men up and down the country are signing for their giros, I'm signing for my fans. Life is sweet, but despite all that, I know I have so much to prove and perhaps tonight is the night when my name will spread further than the comfortable corner of south-west London in which I ply my trade.

Since joining Fulham, I've listened in training, improved, taken my chance in the first-team and I'm now spoken about as a player with potential, a young striker who might go far. Might. That word hangs over me. I don't want might. I'm desperate for success, desperate to be seen as the real deal. Might won't do. Might is for schoolboys. I'm a professional footballer and it is time to prove I'm here to stay.

It's a night match. That makes it even more special. The floodlights shine down on us and I'm ready. Like an actor about to play his first leading role, I step into the spotlight, ready to take centre stage. Don't fluff your lines, Leroy. You've worked too hard to get here.

It's a big match. Bigger than usual. We're away. The stadium isn't like Fulham's Craven Cottage. I love playing there but this is different. More imposing, perhaps more uncomfortable but I can't dwell on the occasion or the crowd.

I bounce gingerly on my toes, nerves and excitement lifting me off the squelchy winter mud. My muscles are well oiled and limber as I nod to the opposing players out of quiet appreciation and professionalism. All I want to hear though is the shriek of the referee's whistle, and get among them, get into them, show them what I can do. Show them that I am ready. Come on, ref, get on with it.

The man in black is talking to the two captains. They shake hands. I'm ten yards away but I can't hear what they're talking about. Thirty odd thousand fans have made sure of that. The noise swirls around my ears filling me with fear and joy in equal measure. I glance over at a mass terrace, fans swaying one way and then the next, seemingly out of sync, but kind of hypnotic to watch. Under the floodlights and in their team's colours, it's like watching colourful algae on a concrete sea.

Most faces are singing, shouting, screaming to raise their heroes and terrify their opponents. The noise pierces through my body but I won't allow myself to buckle. This is it. This is the sort of night we dream of. The captains have finished their formalities and we're ready to go. The crowd's noise gets louder in anticipation, the referee raises his arm to each goalkeeper and the whistle is raised to his mouth. *Get into them, Leroy.* The whistle goes.

I move forward, looking to get amongst their defenders. The 1980s. Defenders aren't graceful playmakers that seem so prevalent in today's more refined game. Tackling from behind is the done thing. Leave your mark. Studs, elbows, foreheads, all tools to be used to gain an advantage. They'll be ready for me. I need to be ready for them, and I am. I'm young, fucking fit, and eager to test myself. *Get into them, Leroy.*

The ball is back with our keeper, he'll kick it long so I position myself, ready to leap, ready to make my first challenge. The ball comes out of the lights, I jump, I get something on it, I feel the force of my opponent on my back, we land. And then it happens.

'You black cunt.'

I'm confused. Did that come from the crowd? It couldn't have. It's too clear. Too close. I look around and my opponent is snarling at me. Hate filling his eyes. It came from him.

I'm momentarily disoriented but the ball breaks free again and it's time to play on. I chase the ball into a channel, grapple with another opponent, my mind again focused on winning the ball, being a dangerous centre-forward. I try to impose myself but the ball is cleared upfield.

'Fucking nigger.'

Another voice. Another player. A different voice but filled with the same venom. I can't believe it. Two players take it in turns to abuse me. After each challenge, every time I turn my back there it is. Abusive comment after abusive comment.

'You black bastard.'

'What are you doing on the same pitch as us, you fucking coon?'

I forget where I am. What I'm supposed to be doing. The wind has been taken out of my enthusiastic sails. I have to get back to doing what I do best, but they have got to me. I'm not naive. I was born and bred in south London. Brixton. I know of racism. I've heard it. I've seen it. This though, this seems different to me. All racism is foul and feral but this is on a football pitch, the place I've always been most at home.

It's not from the terraces either. That I know of. That I'm mentally prepared for. Been on the end of that plenty of times. Fans, their eyes wide with rage and vitriol, spittle flying from their mouths, willing to shout anything to get at you and to convey their hatred for you. This though is from fellow professionals, men I want to compete against tactically and physically, fellow sportsmen I have trained hard to be strong enough to take kicks from, supple enough to out-jump, skilful enough to score goals against.

The game is going on around me but I'm going through the motions. More abuse. What do I say? What do I do? I look at the ref. I'm afraid to say anything to him but maybe he's heard. More abuse but he does nothing. I look to my team-mates? Gordon Davies, my strike partner. He only has eyes (and obviously ears) for the ball, the game. The game that right now I am out of.

It's half-time and we're losing. In our dressing-room, steam rising from our sweaty shirts, the manager, Malcolm Macdonald only talks of a way back into the game. To him, his staff and my team-mates, I have worked manfully and I'm encouraged to do more of the same. More of the same? I'm sure they're right. I'm sure I'm in for more of the same. 'Keep working them, Leroy. Keep trying to stretch them. We'll get back into this.' Stretch them? The only thing that has been stretched out there is my head and no one knows or is it they don't care?

The second half and there's the abuse again. They score again and the game is lost but there is no let-up. 'We've not seen you before,' they say. 'You must've just got off the banana boat.' Their laughter cackles in my ear. They're demeaning me, belittling me, embarrassing me, attacking me all to win a football match. They've set out to wind me up and it has worked. It will be 25 years until I look into the eyes of one of my tormentors and see a glimmer of remorse.

The game passes me by. The whistle goes and I stand alone in the centre of the pitch, splattered in mud, drawing in large, cold breaths of the winter's night. The crowd roar their approval, 21 other players shake hands and share sporting pleasantries. I stand alone. I should be lamenting the result, my poor form, but all I can think of is my two tormentors and the words they've used against me.

They're walking towards me. Smiling. 'Well done, son,' says one of them. 'Better luck next time.'

'Fuck off, you prick,' I say, my voice cracking with emotion. I'm looking him straight in the eye.

'And you,' I say, turning to the other one. 'You can fuck off too.'

They smile. They turn to each other and walk away, like two plump fishermen who have landed the lake's prize carp. Job done and goodnight.

My fists clench up. I want to run behind them and punch them both in the back of their heads. A cowardly but painful act from behind, just like their words were to me. I'm stuck in the mud, momentarily paralysed with my thoughts. I come to. Hitting them won't help. The battle is lost. I trudge from the pitch, forgetting to salute the travelling Fulham fans.

Back in the dressing-room, I'm patted on the back. Apparently a good effort from a young striker. Words of encouragement but they mean nothing. I ignore the inquest to what went wrong. Expletives and what-ifs fill the room but soon the talk is lighter. What pub do we go to, where shall we drown the sorrows? Hammersmith? Yeah, let's get to the Palais. It's agreed.

I'm not interested though. My head is bowed. After what seems an age I undress, grab a towel, wade through the swamp of dirty kit and discarded shin-pads and I'm in the shower. The lads are laughing now. *Win or lose, we're on the booze*. I feel alone.

In a bubble. Unable to talk about what just happened but unable to forget it.

As the steam rises around me I think about it and I think about my reaction. I want to cry. Can't do that. Can't let that happen. Water and steam surround me. Maybe I could let a tear out, no one would know. No, I can't. I'm a footballer. Come on, Leroy.

The players are laughing but I am thinking. Maybe this was the game I had chosen to play. I was a big, athletic centre-forward, taught to get into defenders. *Let them know you're there, Leroy*. Taught to use a shoulder, coached to use my strength if it meant gaining an advantage. *It's part of the game, Leroy*.

Part of the game? Is that what just happened? Is that what I would have to come to terms with? Is that how pros treat other pros, all in the name of winning football matches? Earlier, I said I wasn't naive but maybe I was. I knew I was by no means the first to face such bile from other players and I knew I wouldn't be the last but this had surprised me. Everything I had dreamt of achieving had just been tested.

I leave the ground but have no idea if I can handle this. Suddenly I don't know if I want it. Questions race through my mind and then I think of my dad. 'Keep your powder dry, son.' He always says that to me. I go to bed, thinking about my dad, his journey, his hardships and how he dealt with similar attitudes when he arrived in England; thirty years before but still there.

Football was all I had ever wanted to do and it dawns on me that I won't let those attitudes stop me doing it. I have to find a way to cope. I won't accept it, but I have to deal with it, even use it to better myself. That night as I took to the field, I was a young man with something to prove.

I left as a young *black* man with something to prove.

PART ONE

WILLIE

1

A Quiet Drink

I'VE celebrated scoring a goal at the Kop end at Anfield. I've stood in the centre circle at Upton Park while 25,000 West Ham fans have chanted my name. I've stood on the African west coast, white sand warming my toes as I looked out on the Atlantic Ocean.

All wonderful places but if I shut my eyes and think of a place I have always loved, a place I would always like to be, it would be on my father's knee. Me, a small but proud boy looking up at his smiling face, him a proud dad (I hope!) but for now an entertainer, surrounded by people eagerly awaiting his next line, the next gag within a gag. This is Willie Rosenior, local raconteur, my dad, my first hero. My last hero.

Dad loved to tell stories. Like all the great storytellers, I'm sure only some were true and all were exaggerated but oh, how I loved to be pulled up to his oak-like knees and allowed a ringside seat to his many stories about anything from life back in Sierra Leone to a recent holiday in northern Europe.

It might have only been a few family members, neighbours and friends sitting around us but back then, Dad might as well have sold out Wembley Stadium, such was the joy and pride I took from

23

watching him entertain us all. I might not have understood much of what he was saying and I might have heard the same story for the umpteenth time, but who was counting? Not me. I relished him and his tales and would laugh and laugh every time I heard them. Almost as much as he laughed telling them.

Dad was always laughing, especially when he was telling his own stories. Which is most of the time. He could barely get a sentence out without interrupting himself with the contagious 'hee-hee-hee' chuckle of his.

On so many occasions he would take me from our house in Thornbury Road to the local shops to get a few groceries, and what should have been a 20-minute round trip usually took two hours or more. He sauntered along, stopping to talk to everyone. In conversation, he could switch effortlessly between the Krio language (patois) of his native Sierra Leone, the normal English he speaks to Mum and us kids, and his rather regal, received pronunciation telephone voice – think Philip in *Rising Damp* – depending on his audience.

Dad had an instinct for how to get along with all kinds of people. Princes or paupers, hospitality boxes or terracing, Dad just loved people.

He could be charming, funny, serious, whatever, and people were drawn to him.

* * * * *

Everyone in the area knows Willie Rosenior, and he's got time for anyone that has time for him. Everyone, that is, except for the man from the electricity board when he comes knocking to see if our three-bedroom Victorian house is occupied or not. Then it's a case of, 'Turn the lights off! Turn the lights off! Be quiet!'

Dad is a qualified electrician himself and he's able to rewire the house so when money is short and times are tough, we can avoid the bills. A perk of the job, shall we say. These occasional games of hide-and-seek continue for years, causing amusement and terror in equal measure. It's pretty much the only time our house falls silent.

'It's okay everyone, he's gone, you can come out now.'

Throughout my childhood, it's not unusual for one of Dad's chats during a shopping trip or on the way home from work to lead to an impromptu party back at ours. Any day of the week; whenever Dad feels like it.

The Woodleys who run the paper shop up the road opposite Brixton prison will usually turn up. Chris and Brenda will come round with a huge bowl of chips. They half-fry big batches of them and keep a ready supply in their freezer – so that they only take five minutes to cook when needed. I'm not sure how much time that actually saves, but we normally eat rice at home, so chips are a treat. All the neighbours are welcome to come round. Adults and kids all mixing in.

My mum cooks and, no matter what time of year it is, always insists on getting the coal fire going. She likes the warm glow. Meanwhile, my four elder sisters are in charge of the music, taking their pick from their own LPs – the likes of Earth Wind & Fire, The Jackson Five, Change, Marvin Gaye – and hundreds and hundreds of my dad's records.

My Dad is a music lover and a jazz buff. He played guitar and loved everything from his favourite Ink Spots to Miles Davies, Nat King Col and African High Life. He regularly bought the latest music from a record shop in Brixton market including the popular 'Tighten Up' Reggae albums and Blue Note jazz records.

We all do the 'Car Wash' dance – kick, kick, jump back, jump back, kick, turn, slide, slide. Me and my sisters at the front, Mum, Dad and the neighbours behind, tipsy or drunk, trying to follow the steps.

Parties were frequent in our house. When Mum and Dad didn't have family and neighbours around at our regular 'get togethers', my Dad was to be found most evenings holding court in the kitchen. Although we had set meal times, I was free to eat whenever I was hungry (not a privilege I'm informed enjoyed by my sisters!). Mum always had a huge pot of stew or soup on the stove for unexpected visitors. Mum was extremely resourceful and very versatile, making limited budget go a long way. She could conjure up the most delicious meals from the cheapest cuts from the butchers (beef brisket, neck of lamb, oxtail) or being given away at the butchers (pigs' trotters, chickens' feet). Cooked long and slow until the meat falls off the bone, each one lasts for days. Rice is reheated until all that's left at the bottom of the pan is as hard as a biscuit, and we eat it like one. Nothing is wasted. Not with Mum at the helm.

It is the kitchen rather than the living room where my sisters and I always congregate to listen to Dad's life stories. I sit on his lap. My sisters sit on chairs scattered about the room or on the floor. Mum is buzzing around in the background, chipping in with the odd comment, usually to wind him up. Even those stories he has told again and again, he always finds a new way to tell them. It's far more entertaining than watching the three channels on telly.

One evening in 1970, with six-year-old me perched on that knee, he launches into a story with all his familiar gusto, but hold on, this is one he's never told us before, 'It was one evening in November back in 1954. I was 25 at the time, a trainee electrician. I joined my mates for a quiet drink after work down at The George in Tooting – it's still there now. We were all black guys – the black guys that came to this country at the time, we all tended to stick together.

'One of the guys was with his girlfriend. A white girl. I'd only known her a little while. Bit shorter than me – about five-foot-eight, slim with short mousey brown hair. Tight-fitting knee-length pink coat zipped up to her neck. Black boots reaching up just below the knee. A few guys in the pub noticed her when she walked in. Hee-hee-hee.'

Mum shoots him a mock quizzical look.

'Hee-hee. Yes, very attractive, but nothing on you, dear. Hee-hee-hee. And I was looking pretty sharp myself. Nice black overcoat, dark brown suit, crisp white shirt and a black tie. But I was chatting to her, not chatting her up – as I say, she was my friend's girlfriend. I talk to everyone. And she was a nice girl. So we're sitting having a drink, talking, laughing, when these three Teddy Boys – teenagers, who'd been standing at the bar – came over. All tall, white; quiffs as tight as their drainpipe trousers. I hadn't noticed, but apparently they'd been watching us ever since they saw Sarah join our crowd.

'I say, [Dad puts on his best telephone voice] "Gentlemen."

'The men ignore me and look over at Sarah.

'One says, "What are you doing?"

'"Pardon me?" she replies.

'"What the heck are you doing with them?" (I'm pretty sure 'heck' is not the word the man actually used.)

'So I say, [telephone voice, again] "Excuse me chaps, you don't need to be talking to a lady like that."

He starts giggling again, 'All hell breaks loose! Hee-hee-hee. These boys are going crazy! Hee-hee. They're punching the hell out of me and the other guys. I'm trying to defend myself when – thud! I feel a heavy whack on the side of my head.'

Dramatic pause. My sisters and I are all looking at him agog.

'Hee-Hee. One of them had hit me with a beer bottle – knocked me over! Hee-hee-hee.'

He's chuckling away to himself. I'm looking up at him, half-horrified and half-smiling at his jovial description of the incident.

'Why are you laughing?' says Mum, sitting down next to him, then turning to my sisters. 'He could have died, you know. They found a shard of glass this close to his temple,' she continues, gesturing with the tips of her thumb and forefinger almost touching. 'He spent weeks in hospital.'

'Hee-hee-hee, luckily St George's hospital was just around the corner. We were clever. We drank in a pub near accident and emergency! And anyway, I'm still here, aren't I?' Dad continued to tell an enthralled crowd about his lying on the floor, rushing blood ruining his always immaculate attire.

The fight continued around him, spilling out on to the street. The sight of white teenagers and a group of black youths would soon be commonplace in England's cities, especially London, but the thought of some customers just sitting there and finishing their pints like this was a bit of Saturday afternoon sport is a galling one.

My dad is left dazed on the sticky wooden floor of the pub, gasping for breath, arching his back as he reached to try and stem the flow of blood, while the fighting between his friends and the Teddy Boys spilled on to the street, the locals enjoying their afternoon beverages seemingly oblivious to Dad's plight.

'I remember one guy going to the loo with the fight going on and man, the smell when they opened the door to those toilets. Hee-hee. It was like smelling salts! That woke me up! Hee-hee-hee.'

Other punters were coolly asking questions about how the whole thing started, insinuating that maybe my dad had it coming to him. Soon phone calls were made and the small matter of the glass sticking out of my dad's bloody face was dealt with by the arrival of an ambulance. It was serious. Dad removed and in an ambulance, the mess was cleaned up from the pub's sticky floorboards, arrests were made and medics got on with saving a life. With that smile on his face, Dad described to us all in technicolour tones, the crimson ambulance pillow and how he was immediately wheeled through to the operating theatre, and – like the audience listening to this story – all anyone could do was wait.

Such was the severity of his injury, Dad was kept in hospital for weeks for observation. Now, the inch-long scar by his temple – which he takes great pleasure in showing us – is there for all of us to see. A badge of honour. Welcome to England.

* * * * *

I thought a lot about that story. Later I would face racial abuse and while I was never physically hurt, I know what it is to feel alone while it is happening. It will be a long time before I fully understand.

This was a working-class south London neighbourhood – a white working-class south London neighbourhood – in 1954. People were more interested in finishing their pints and then heading home to get dressed up for a night out. Maybe dancing at the Brixtoria Ballroom Club on the Stockwell Road or the Wimbledon Palais; or going to the flicks at the Mayfair Cinema on Upper Tooting Road; or checking their numbers at the local bingo hall.

It was just nine years since the end of the Second World War when Britain – and London especially – was still trying to heal itself from the scars of the conflict. In July 1944, a bomb had dropped on the corner of Idlecombe and Southcrofts roads nearby, wiping the place out. Post-war, some families responded by moving out to places like Devon or Salisbury in Wiltshire. Other more defiant types were adamant that they wouldn't be forced out. Then the perceived threat was no longer from above but from outsiders who – in the eyes of the vast majority – were trying to change their British way of life.

Young black men were seen as a threat, no matter how personable they were. No wonder the drinkers around my dad didn't want to get involved. No wonder they didn't want to get blood on their hands.

* * * * *

'I was in hospital for weeks and the police managed to find the guys who attacked me,' Dad continues. 'They were arrested and taken into custody. And they were all facing a long time in prison for attempted murder.

'Ahead of the trial, the mother of the boy who actually hit me with the bottle comes to visit me. She wants to distance herself from what her son has done and apologise for the unprovoked attack.

'I could tell she was sincere and she came to see me regularly during my recovery. She asked me to forgive her boy.

'By the time the case went to court, it was a big story in the area. Big story – the *South London Press* was all over it. Hee-hee-hee. In the courtroom, when the defence lawyer stands up, he tucks his left thumb in his waistcoat and waves his right hand around like a Shakespearean actor as he speaks to the judge.

'"I am going to try and keep this very simple for Mr Rosenior," he says, "because he has come from the Colonies and obviously doesn't have the language to deal with this sort of thing."

'Hee-hee, that's what he said. He carries on talking for a while, outlining the case. He's talking as if I'm not there. I just sit there listening, looking like this.' (Dad pulls a face of fake bewilderment.) When the two of them have finished, I stand up.'

He turns on his telephone voice.

'"Please do excuse me, Your Honour," I say. "I was brought up with English as my first language. I went to St Edward's, an English grammar school and I am perfectly capable of speaking the language, possibly even more fluently than you, sir. So, please, if you could refer directly to me with any questions, I would be most grateful."

'"Hee-hee-hee – mouths dropped around that court. Stunned silence! After that the judge spoke to me on level terms, and when it came to summing up he asked if I had anything else to say.

"Yes, Your Honour, I would like to make a plea for leniency for the young man who struck me with the bottle. His mother has come to see me, we have struck up a friendship and I feel that he wants to change. His mother is going to play a big part in that so I ask for clemency."

'The judge, the defence lawyer and probably half the courtroom can't believe it. Hee-hee-hee.'

* * * * *

There was my dad fighting the corner of a guy who had nearly killed him.

'The judge says to me, "Mr Rosenior, if more people had your attitude, Britain would be a better place."'

This is a story that Dad will enjoy repeating over the years. Like all good raconteurs, he'll tweak the details here and there – I still reckon he might have made that bit up about the judge praising him! However, the truth remains that, due to my dad's intervention, his attacker got a very lenient sentence for his crime, just 18 months. His mother personally thanked Dad afterwards, but he just told her to forget about it and make sure she looked after her son.

But why does a father tell his six-year-old son and four young daughters such a gory tale, even if it is laced with humour? Well, he has reasons. I learn that everything my father says to us is for a reason. And the underlying lessons of this anecdote will only truly become clear to me when racism impacts on my own life. Fifty years later though I still chuckle at the judge's words. He was right. People like my dad did make Britain a better place.

2

Willie and Gladys

No Irish, No Blacks, No Dogs

I T'S a frequent and definite sign that greeted visitors to many of London's post-war public houses and lodgings but, fortunately for Gladys and Willie's impending nuptials, it did not sway in the window of Wandsworth's grand old town hall on an unseasonably warm October Saturday afternoon in 1955.

Just days earlier, Willie, knowing he was to leave London to start his national service, got down on one knee and asked Gladys to be his wife. She of course accepted and in doing so agreed to marry into the Royal Air Force. Willie was to be posted away on the Monday, so told Gladys – whom he had been seeing for almost a year – to have her best clothes on that Saturday and to join him at the town hall, where, to steal a south London phrase, they would get 'hitched'.

So Gladys, in her favourite dress, and Willie, in his best suit, walked into the fairly new art deco building and stood in front of the registrar ready to start a life as man and wife. 'And where is your witness?' said an officious- looking gentleman, his eyes peering over his spectacles like a frustrated owl tolerating a couple of playful bunnies.

'My what?' said Willie.

'Your witness. You certainly can't get married without a witness.'

'We don't have one,' said Willie.

'Well you had better go and get one then,' said the registrar.

'You mean, it can be anyone?'

The registrar nodded and with that Willie told Gladys not to move and rushed out of the room before coming back just minutes later with a friendly-looking Irishman. 'Here's my witness,' he said. Formalities were concluded and with that Gladys and Willie became Gladys and Willie Rosenior, my mum and dad.

It turned out that Dad had sprinted out of the hall, on to the street, and asked a kind-looking gentleman if could assist him and his fiancee. After the ceremony the newlyweds took the man to the nearest pub where they thanked him with a pint and went on their merry way.

A year later, the couple had another more formal wedding at the Holy Trinity Church in Tooting, where Gladys looked radiant in her white dress and there was no need for impromptu witnesses. Winston Churchill had recently resigned as Prime Minister and frequent smog kept London under a dense blanket that did little to lift the city's gloom, even if over a decade had passed since the end of the Second World War.

To us Roseniors, who are the product of that funny afternoon in Wandsworth, Mum and Dad's story is a romantic and momentous one. A young lady and young man, born and raised in the same city, Freetown in Sierra Leone, having never met, travel to London, England, the capital of the diminishing British Empire, are introduced, start to see more of each other, face the prejudices of their new world together, dance together, fall in love, get married, have a family and set up the most wonderful of homes.

Not that my mum came looking for love. The promise of work in the fledgling NHS was her calling. A good student in Freetown, she had done well with her education, passing her British exams at school and deciding that England was where her future lay. On arrival, she settled as well as a young lady thousands of miles from home, friends and family could, but after 18 months at Barnet General Hospital she decided to pursue medicine, which meant a stint back at technical college where she would take a science qualification.

Mum then was busy but Dad being Dad, his route to England's mountains green was a little less straightforward. Born in 1929, Dad was named Willie after his grandfather who died the year he was born.

Born out of wedlock as his father, a mere undertaker and not seen as the social or economic equal to his mother, Willie Rosenior was a bright and adventurous boy who did well at school and loved sports (especially football and cricket) but like so many of his generation, his wanderlust would see him move away from his home in Freetown and discover the world beyond.

For a good year Dad was missing, assumed God knows what after he packed his bags, got himself a canoe and headed for Senegal. It was a treacherous journey up the Atlantic coast but one he managed and with a good grasp of French having studied it at school he found work at an airport hotel, saving his salary for more adventures to come.

Having put his family's mind at rest by returning to Freetown, in 1953 he was off again, this time for France where he made a living working in Paris restaurants and playing his jazz guitar on its busy and bohemian streets. Soon though, London beckoned. His uncle Bob was living there and having heard about his busking nephew, he thought a call to England would be best. The Commonwealth Office granted the request and Dad (and his guitar) headed across the Channel.

Dad's first residence was at 4 Thornbury Road, the street on which we would all one day live. His uncle left for Africa but he stayed on in the flat owned by the Korns, a lovely German couple, and was looked after by the Youngs, a couple my mother knew from Freetown who moved in downstairs. Mr Young was in London to complete his law degree in Lincoln's Inn and the couple loved to throw dinner parties and it was through his new neighbours that Willie met Gladys.

> 'I used to visit the Youngs frequently. On the days of the dinners I used to go to number three Thornbury Road from college to do Mrs Young's hair. That's how Willie and I used to meet. Mrs Young had taken him under her wing, preparing meals for him. By then he was working at Mullards Radio Valve Co making valves for TVs in Mitcham and studying Electrical Engineering at Wandsworth College. I was scared of him when I first met him. He seemed much older than he was. He was always in this long trench coat and soon he would walk me to the bus stop and offer me 50p for my fare. I had been taught not to take money from strange men though and politely declined.'
>
> ***Gladys Rosenior***

Dad was besotted and soon they were spending their Saturday nights together at the local cinema or better still, dancing at the dance halls of Hammersmith or Streatham, where his moves impressed a slowly smitten Gladys.

In fact dancing was something they would love to do together for the rest of their lives.

> 'I only gave it up when he died.'
>
> ***Gladys Rosenior***

So Willie and Gladys were very much a couple, 'courting' as they called it back then, but things got serious when she moved in with him to a flat on Crockerton Road. Yes, this was very much a London couple. Well, kind of. They'd left behind the hustle and bustle of Freetown for the even busier streets of England's capital. Separately they had known their home town, a thriving port, once the capital of British West Africa and home to the descendants of many liberated slaves in the 1830s.

The city, on a peninsula, is ringed by the whitest of white sandy beaches, markets are teaming with life and temperatures flirt with 40 degrees in the hottest of months between February and April. London must have been so different for these two young people lured by the promise of perceived Western prosperity.

> 'It was so strange when I arrived. I was a young lady miles from home. The weather was fine. In fact it was nice to wrap up in long coats and fashionable scarves. No, it was the strange glances from people that I remember. The part of south London that I came to was starting to be home to people from all over the Commonwealth and the SS *Empire Windrush* had made its famous journey from the Caribbean in 1948, but still, black faces were very much the minority.'
>
> ***Gladys Rosenior***

In the early 1950s there was the promise of plenty of work, especially on the expanding transport networks or in the new NHS, but housing was a problem and families arriving in England were crammed into the smallest of flats or bedsits. My own family were packed into a small flat when I was a toddler but in the 1950s tensions were starting to rise and the restless natives were becoming more than simply curious about these new guests from the colonies.

'At first, people were fascinated by us. I'd be sitting on the bus, and someone would sit next to me and pick up my hand, and run my black skin to see if the colour would come off. That was odd. I remember walking home one day and seeing a black man. I went over and started talking to him. It was so unusual to see another black face that you had to stop and have a chat. It soon got nastier though and you noticed people crossing the road or saying unfriendly things.'

Gladys Rosenior

Having chosen engineering as his future career, Dad had had thoughts of moving back to France and even Sierra Leone but having met Gladys, his thoughts turned to settling down and a life in the services and the RAF. He was posted in Somerset, Lincolnshire and Suffolk, so my mum was a frequent visitor and with the start of a one day large family, they settled into military life.

In 1958, Dad, a keen amateur footballer and fan, turned on his wireless to be greeted by the news that a plane carrying Matt Busby's young Manchester United team home from a European Cup tie in Yugoslavia had crashed in Germany. Like much of the country, the Busby Babes had caught Dad's imagination. This youthful and vibrant side was a flickering light in foggy post-war England but it had been extinguished and together, like so many families around the nation, my parents mourned. Dad, a serviceman with a wife and young family, was sitting by his wireless in his Lincolnshire RAF base, awaiting more news about a beloved football team from England's north-west.

Mum even won a bit of cash on the football pools, not loads but enough to buy the young family their first car. However, for all of their integration, down on the streets of London, local gangs of youths were beginning to stir at the thought of these *others* making England their home permanently.

What had begun in London's Notting Hill Gate as individual incidents of black men being attacked by small groups of white teenagers escalated until one night in August 1958 when a more organised, angrier group made their way down the streets of this then run-down part of town. One writer at the time described it as, 'A crowd of a thousand white men and some women…tooled up with razors, knives, bricks and bottles.'

The trouble occurred nightly, culminating with an incident on 1 September near to and on the Portobello Road with groups of guys going on the rampage, planning on beating up any black man they came across whilst women hung out of their windows screaming, 'Go on boys, get yourselves some blacks.' Race riots had arrived in London.

That night though, large groups of black men had waited and as their would-be attackers strode purposefully down the street shouting 'let's burn the niggers out', they were greeted by opposing gangs, equally as angry and equally as 'tooled up'. The tinder beneath London's streets may have been lit but for my mum and dad in leafy Lincolnshire, him with his starchy uniform to keep pressed and her with her house and young daughter to care for, life was far less volatile.

After four years of Dad in the Air Force, the family moved back to the capital. The fire from those Notting Hill riots hadn't spread but there was of course an undercurrent of racial mistrust and tension. My dad had continued his studies as an engineer and soon got work in a local factory and one guy at his work was the less cultured type and most days, Dad would be on the end of this man's racial slurs.

As mentioned, Dad could and would smile in the face of most ill-tempered adversaries but this was getting on his nerves. Now skilled in his chosen profession, Dad managed to rig a machine used by this guy so that it would dish out a small electric shock. 'Just a small one,' Willie would laugh when recounting the story.

It turned out the 'small' electric shock fused the man's two fingers together so that he had webbed fingers for the rest of his life. Worse still, Karen's (my teenage girlfriend and future wife) father knew the guy and I swore the family to secrecy so as not to antagonise my would-be father-in-law. The guy deserved it though!

So, having mastered (perhaps too much) his trade, Dad settled into a small flat in Brixton with his hard-working wife and growing family. Each morning, he and my mum would draw their curtains and, while they must have often longed for the warm familiarity of their Freetown home, got on with the job of clothing and feeding their English-born children.

Here's to Willie and Gladys.

3

Brixton Academy

I'M on the 220 bus, sitting on the top deck but feeling on top of the world. We creep through south-west London. Plush houses, the river, rowing clubs, affluence. We cross Putney Bridge and stop in the afternoon traffic. I turn to my left and there, looming over Bishops Park and the murky, brown Thames are four floodlights.

Football people from anywhere in the word will understand that feeling we all get when we see floodlights. A sense of anticipation. All you have to do is turn those things on and something special can happen. Soon something special will happen there for me. Excitement wells in my stomach.

That's how I felt as I sat on that bus one afternoon in late 1982, staring at Fulham's Craven Cottage with silent anticipation.

The bus moves on towards home. Through Wandsworth, into Tooting. Now I'm near the spot where my young dad was beaten up to within an inch of his wonderful life. Ignorant, scared, young white boys hadn't liked his kind laughing with their women. Now, 30 years later, his son is eager to get home and tell him the big news.

My stop now and I'm gingerly walking towards my street. Our street. Not breaking into a run, no need, let's not get too excited, a fast walk will do. Eager. On my street now. Get the key out, get in. Tell everyone.

Home. It was everything to me for so long. The front hall, the living room to the left, the kitchen down the hall. Always something going on, always something cooking – both in the culinary *and* metaphorical sense. 30 Thornbury Road. A terraced house in south London but to me, for so long, it was Piccadilly bloody Circus. And I loved it.

We had moved to the house on the very street that had played such a big part in my mum and dad's life when I was five. It was here that Dad had lived and met Mum and it was here that my four sisters and I laughed, argued, learnt and lived. My world didn't stretch far in terms of square mileage but growing up, it seemed a vast kingdom, full of magical people from all walks of life.

Our street was at the back of Brixton Prison. It's an imposing, gothic, Victorian building, designed to frighten those who arrive at its gates but in many ways it was a reassuring presence in my young life. Acting like a garden fence, the prison was a natural boundary.

I didn't even know that Brixton Hill – the road on which the prison entrance sits – existed until I went to secondary school and that road was part of my commute in.

No, life in my youngest days were joyous, almost idyllic. Doors were often left open, neighbours were neighbourly and laughter seemed to fill the four walls in which I lived. According to my mum, I came into this world amid joyous tones.

Monday 24 August 1964, and on hearing that his sixth child was – at last – a boy, my dad ran around the corridors of Weir Hospital in Balham; me, swaddled in his arms, him running around as if at Wembley doing a lap of honour holding the FA Cup, and telling anyone who would listen, 'It's a boy, a boy, it's a boy!' Not that my four sisters took offence. All dressed up in their Sunday best, they followed him reiterating the news by telling bemused onlookers, 'We have a brother! We have a brother!' Willie Leroy Rosenior was born.

Away from my excited family, the world is a traumatic but exciting place. America is sending more and more troops to Vietnam, sparking mass protests on the nation's streets and university campuses. Cassius Clay – for whose life that conflict will play such a big part – has defeated the mighty Sonny Liston in Miami and has changed his name to Muhammad Ali. Soon, in that summer's Tokyo Olympics, a super-heavyweight called Joe Frazier will win gold, taking him on a collision course with Ali that will shudder the world of boxing right down to its boots.

Sidney Poitier has become the first black man to win an Academy Award as Best Actor for his role in *Lilies of the Field*. Months later Nelson Mandela and seven others are sentenced to life in prison and sent to Robben Island in South Africa.

At home The Beatles have flown the nest and are dazzling America with their floppy-haired brilliance. Not interested in the Fab Four, Mods and Rockers are spending the summer beating each other up on the beaches of south-east England.

Weeks after my arrival, in the General Election, an unofficial slogan for a Tory candidate in Smethwick in the West Midlands reads, 'If you want a nigger for your neighbour, vote Labour.' The Tories won that seat but Labour took the election.

The day I'm born, Manfred Mann are top of the pops with 'Do Wah Diddy Diddy', keeping The Beatles' 'Hard Day's Night' off the number one spot. The Searchers, The Rolling Stones, The Animals, The Kinks, Cilla Black and Dusty Springfield all dominate the top 20. Sean Connery will soon star in his third Bond movie, *Goldfinger*. Yes, Britain is chilling nicely and soon Cool Britannia will rule the waves.

Two days before my birth, BBC2 (itself only months old) airs a new show called *Match of the Day*. Tellingly for my own future, the first goal scored on the highlights programme is from Liverpool's Roger Hunt. Every bit a number nine.

Liverpool goals, African American actors and scooter-riding rioters; none were on my doorstep when I was growing up in our first house in Talma Road in Brixton. Ours was a small place, very small when you factor in five children sharing a room. The toilet was of the outdoor variety and late at night, with the neighbours' vicious dog vociferously opposed to those who used it, this toddler was simply not going to. It was an unfortunate decision for one of my sisters who woke one morning next to me and the evidence in my pyjamas (hanging from my backside like a tail) that I had stayed put. I wasn't a popular room-mate that day!

In my home I was known by my middle name, Leroy, and once I became a footballer I would hide the fact that my real given christian name was Willie, for obvious reasons. In fact my own children only found out recently and laughed that on my birth certificate it is Willie – not William – that I am registered as.

My first memory is from the back of a police car and I'm only three years old. No, I hadn't been enticed into an early life of crime, but I had managed to stroll out of my house and explore the surrounding streets without my parents knowing. To be fair to my mum, she was working while my dad, who was working nights, looked after me. He must have been tired because it was a while before anyone knew I was gone.

> 'Leroy's dad called me to say that our son had disappeared. Disappeared! I remember all the family walking the streets trying to find him. My daughters all thought they'd never see their brother again, but we stayed calm, and eventually a blue lady – that's what we called policewomen – found him and drove him home.'
>
> **Gladys Rosenior, Leroy's mum**

That early wanderlust wouldn't be an everyday trait. Leaving home, after all, seemed futile when there was always so much going on, so much fun being had by my family and a constant stream of visitors. Life at 30 Thornbury Road was lively to say the least. Five kids, my mum, my dad and an open door policy to neighbours and friends eager to join those impromptu parties.

First of all the kitchen. My dad was a wonderful cook, but the kitchen was my mum's domain. Dad would take one of his two-hour strolls to the local shops and come back with the ingredients that Mum would cook. Chickens were picked out alive in Brixton market, then killed by the butcher before being taken home by Mum, where she would burn off their feathers. I always remember the smell of those burning feathers. It was like burning flesh! Never mind, she'd then scrape them off with a sharp knife and boil the whole bird. It was all used, including the feet.

They were delicacies, as were all parts of a pig. Mum always said that English people didn't know how to appreciate a whole animal and would get cuts like pig trotters and ears (now very fashionable) from our local butcher who happily kept them aside for her.

Having scalded the birds in a huge pot to remove all the feathers, mum would use her inventive culinary skills to create seasoning closest to her Krio recipes and would let the meat marinate for at least 24 hours before cooking it slowly so that it would melt from the bone on to your tongue. I'm getting hungry just thinking about it as the memory of that smell – the smell of my childhood – fills my nostrils.

Maybe at the time I took that culinary brilliance for granted. Being so far away from home with little access to traditional ingredients, Mum performed miracles which were appreciated by visiting Sierra Leonean family and English neighbours who were always eager to try out her delicious dishes and where always the first in line to get served! Amongst them were our good friends and neighbours, Chris and Brenda, always had frozen food in their freezer and it fascinated me. They would cook and freeze and defrost, often bringing their food over and I must admit, the idea of fish fingers and chips was always so appealing to me as it was not something we ate regularly.

Dad was a true people person, he cared passionately about people and the need to look out for those less fortunate in society. He often lamented and despaired at 'Man's inhumanity to man' and believed that there was more that united people than separated them. Mum and Dad were often approached advice and guidance by family and friends, a role which they filled very naturally.

Dad was also an African to his core, a Krio boy from the East End of Freetown – proud of his heritage. He often described Freetown as being the 'Athens of West Africa' in its hey day.

Coming from a well-respected family Dad enjoyed early privileges including being the first boy in the neighbourhood to own a bike. Despite this comfortable life he had a thirst for adventure and an aversion to the prospect of becoming an accountant in his Uncle Bob's bank. Too boring a fate for a frustrated jazz guitarist!

This propelled Dad to run away to Dakar, Senegal, where he made friends with 'Siddy' who later invited him to Paris. He was to discover that 'Siddy' was in fact Cheikh Anta Diop, at the time Africa's leading scholar and a famous historian, anthropologist, physicist, and politician who studied the human race's origins and pre-colonial African culture. The University in Dakar is named after him.

Dad would talk animatedly about his Paris days where after work with 'Siddy' they explored the jazz clubs and bars, eating good food, listening to great jazz and heatedly discussing life and politics!

Alas it was not to last! Dad was eventually tracked down (and relieved of his occasional busking sessions in Paris) by a posse of uncles and unceremoniously repatriated to Freetown, from where he subsequently travelled to the UK.

This is an example of how Dad could effortlessly relate to everyone – from the most accomplished academic to women selling fish in the markets of Freetown where incidentally he was, of course, a favoured customer, joking with and charming the venders who were quick to reserve the catch of the day for him at a bargain price! This was a habit he continued in the UK notably with shopkeepers and the traders in Brixton market, some of whom remember him still today. A true man of the people!

Dad would return from the shops with ingredients but also with some people he'd met along the way and the party was soon getting started. The folding doors in the living room turned two rooms into one and with food and drinks prepared, the fire was lit and the festivities would get under way.

Music played a big part in our house. My cousin Keith was Stevie Wonder's manager when he was touring the UK, so his music was often on. My sister started DJing too and plenty of shelf space in the living room was reserved for 12-inch vinyl. As drinks started to flow, us kids would put on 'Car Wash' and try to teach the adults – white and black – the moves to the famous song.

We'd all line up, my sisters and me knowing the moves off by heart, as the adults joined in, more enthusiastic than efficient but laughter would fill the house.

'Ooh ooh
You might not ever get rich
But let me tell ya it's better than diggin' a ditch
There ain't no tellin' who you might meet
A movie star or maybe even an Indian chief'

The lyrics seemed appropriate. This wasn't a rich home, but it was better than digging a ditch and you certainly never knew who you might meet. I can't say we ever had a movie star in or an

Indian chief, but life was varied and while I didn't ever hear the word 'multicultural', I guess that's exactly what my childhood was.

While we didn't have movie stars or Indian chiefs over, I did have a connection to a superstar in my childhood. Paul Gadd was my best mate from an early age and the eagle-eyed among you will notice he shares his name with his father, who was better known as Gary Glitter. Paul was a regular at my house. His mum and dad had separated when we were young, but his dad, a superstar in the 1970s, would often visit and it wasn't hard to know when he did. All you needed to do was look out for the big silver Rolls-Royce and a man in a matching fur coat.

Paul and I were inseparable. We had very different upbringings; his had obviously become very plush. His dad was *the* biggest pop star in the country in the early to mid-1970s and he had the trinkets that went along with that fame and fortune. He would wear the best clothes, and have the best toys, steak for his supper but there was something he loved about my house, the love and the real camaraderie – as well as Mum's chicken – that money couldn't buy.

We would spend hours building go-carts from two planks of wood, some wheels from some discarded pram, some rope and a bolt. Ingenious really. We used to dart along our streets at quite a pace but soon discovered bikes. Paul had a Chopper, an icon of 1970s engineering. I got the Tomahawk, its cheaper and much smaller brother. Aged 12, we attempted to ride to Brighton. There he was on his cool, red bike and there I was, my knees almost hitting my ears every time I pedalled. We didn't get far.

We also had a Gary Glitter tribute act! I'm not sure such a thing would go down too well these days but we were very popular at school. The 'Junior Glitter Band' as we were known, would put on shows and concerts at school, gaining quite a local following with our cover versions. I guess if a singer's son can't nail his songs, no one can.

My friendship with Paul, like most pre-teen unions, seemed like it would never end but growing up can ruin the best of things. Our break-up came at The Strand grammar school that both of us had gone to after primary. I had passed the 11-plus but Paul had struggled. Such though was our friendship a case was made to the school that we should stay together and so Paul came along with me.

One day, walking from one class to another, Paul and I were having an argument. I can't recall what it was over but there we were in this grand old Victorian building arguing like an old married couple, and Paul – from nowhere – called me a 'nig-nog'. Now I had heard kids at school say the odd thing to the odd person, jokes were made in playgrounds, but this was different. This wasn't a joke. He meant it. I could see it in his screwed up eyes. I'm not saying Paul had become a card-holding racist overnight but something was different.

Television sitcoms like *Love Thy Neighbour* were on back then, so Paul might joke with me about being black this and black that, but that's all they were, jokes. On this occasion, he used the term 'nig-nog' with malice as if it was a way of getting at me and upsetting me. It worked.

I flipped. Bang, I hit him. Suddenly we were fighting on the stairs, grappling and throwing teenage shots at each other. Put it this way, I didn't lose. No one saw us fighting so we weren't punished, but Paul walked out of the school gates and didn't come back. I told my dad what had happened and he was disappointed that a close friendship had ended. He understood why I had struck out but was calm, simply saddened by a good friendship gone.

After that, Paul left and went to Italia Conti performing arts school and we stopped seeing each other for about 20 years. A decade that had started with the break-up of The Beatles and now this was the end of the Junior Glitter Band. British music was taking heavy blows!

I thought a lot about Paul over the years. He continued to come over to see my mum and dad when I wasn't there as he always felt close to them. His dad hadn't been around for him and while on the outside, Paul had everything a superstar father could offer, mine was the far richer household.

We would go to Gary Glitter's new home in Surrey after he split with Paul's mum and yes, there was the pool and the big rooms (and in hindsight the very young girlfriends) but that isn't what a kid really needs. Twenty years later, we would meet up as he lived in the West Country, where we would make up and we laughed about those great old days.

When the news broke about Gary Glitter's crimes, I was sad for Paul. Not because he might have been in danger, I'm sure he wasn't, but because he had had such a hard upbringing dealing with a famous but distant dad.

Standing on the stairs with Paul, I was overcome with anger. I had cracked and lashed out. As ever, it was my dad who managed to calm me down.

Dad had a steely manner. He would smile and he would laugh – a lot – but he would never flinch from facing up to life's problems. Problems though, to Dad, were not insurmountable hindrances there only to paralyse you. Meet anything with positivity and any problem could be made to go away.

That's what Dad had. Positivity. In abundance. If positivity was a commodity you could buy and sell, it would have been him with the big Rolls-Royce and the fur coat. We never had a Roller but one story about Dad underlines just how he looked upon life.

Dad used to always drive the family to Belgium for our holidays and one year we were going in a new motor. Dad – in all his wisdom – bought an old Austin Cambridge for £10 from his best friend, a guy called Paddy who worked for Lambeth Council (I never knew if Paddy was short for Patrick or just the usual nickname because he was Irish). To be fair, it was a lovely car, wood panelling, matching wooden bench seats.

It was a big old three-litre car, fitting seven of us in comfortably, and to be fair it got us all to Belgium. We had our holiday and we drove back some of the way but at Dover, nothing. The car simply wouldn't start. My mum was tutting and scowling at her husband but all he did was smile, open the door, and give the car a little tap on the roof as if proudly acknowledging one of his kids, and said, 'What a car, it got us this far didn't it? What a great little car.'

He then strolled off and in no time at all, he came back in a different car and we drove home.

> 'We were always the family pushing a car somewhere with dad smiling at the front. It was so embarrassing. We were a big family so us sisters would be crammed in the back, while Leroy sat at the front, straddling the gear stick!'
>
> **Lynda Rosenior, Leroy's sister**

Once, while in the RAF, Dad was supposed to get in a plane. Mum was at home, heavily pregnant, so his commanding officers gave Dad permission to go home. The plane that Dad would have been in crashed, killing the poor man who had taken his place. 'That was lucky,' he would always say, seemingly unaware of his understatement. That was my father. Faced with a problem, just smile, think and move on. It was a trait that, once I was a young black footballer trying to make my way in the early 1980s, I would gladly and necessarily inherit, but I think all of Dad's kids took much of that positivity into their adult lives.

My sisters are all wonderful, strong women. They remain my best friends and that's despite them all dressing me up in little girls' clothes and using me as their little human doll when we were kids. I adore them all.

My eldest, Lauren, was the first black head girl at her school, St Martins-in-the-Fields in Tulse Hill, near Brixton. She went on to do a Masters and became an engineer, and while working for Mars she created a machine to make Maltesers. She basically adapted a cement mixer to make the small drops of chocolate. Incredible really, especially if you meet her as she isn't the sharpest!

Then there's Lynda, Lorna and Lena (Mum and Dad liked the Ls) but between Lena and me, Mum had a stillborn girl called Lisa. Lisa wasn't talked about much but I know my parents thought about her a lot, although who knows if they would have had me, had she survived.

What I do know is my sisters were fantastic role models; confident, intelligent and outspoken. I love them all and have them to thank for keeping me grounded even when I was becoming a recognised professional footballer.

'Leroy is very purposeful. He doesn't talk for the sake of talking and I think he got that from being the youngest boy with four sisters. He learned to choose his moments as a kid. His talent for football wasn't a big part of the household but I do recall the freezing mornings on Clapham Common. We would all go over there and support him. It was probably quite lonely for Leroy. None of us were into football, so he had to be focused and put in the hours on his own.'

Lynda Rosenior

Into my teens, sport was becoming more and more important in my life. It was cricket in the summer and football all year round. I'd be lying though if I said that I had all the sporting bragging rights in the house. Lynda was a brilliant sprinter and hurdler, running at a decent level and she gave me a slight lesson one day on our way home.

I could run. I liked to sprint. I remember one day running full pelt for a bus – the old Routemasters with no doors – near Herne Hill. It was a good race and I just got on it as it was moving off at a pace. The bus conductor looked me up and down, whistled and said, 'Fuckin' hell, son. You can run.' Soon though Lynda would prove otherwise.

Walking along the pavement, off Kingswood Road, around the corner from home, she said, 'Come on, Leroy, let's have a race.' I chuckled thinking here we go, easy. Off we go and, we're neck and neck and then my sister puts on the burners and it was all technique. The arms started to pump and she simply lifted her knees and she was gone. Lesson learnt, both in technique and in underestimating my sisters.

Football was of course my big passion. I love cricket and was a very good wicketkeeper as I had good reactions, but it was football that I excelled in. As a young boy I would spend hours with a balloon, throwing it up, and learning to jump and hang in the air so I could head it. That's where I became decent at heading, I think. I was never the tallest centre-forward (not even 6ft) but I could jump and I could stay jumped.

My primary school teacher, Mr Harris, had played youth level football and he saw something in me, encouraging me to play the game. At secondary school, despite being the youngest in my year, I was standing out and I remember one kid, a guy called Mensah Offei. He was the hardest kid at school, no one messed with him, but after one lunchtime game he took me aside and said, 'Leroy, you're good, do you know that?' They were simple words but they resonated with me. I wasn't the loudest kid around or flash or anything like that but I had a talent and it was being recognised.

'I met Leroy at The Strand, a secondary school near Brixton. I remember the first day. He walked into the classroom, the only one wearing the school cap! He looked hilarious and took the appropriate amount of grief for it. The cap didn't last long but the friendship did.'

Martin Loveday, Leroy's schoolboy friend

In the early 1980s there was racial tension in south London but I only noticed it on a small scale. I was playing for a local club, Old Grammarians near Wandsworth Common, and was with a team-mate on the bus to a game. On the bus with us was this shaven-haired guy with 'SLF' written on the back of his jacket. My mate, who was white, wasn't having that. 'That's South London Front, Leroy,' he said. 'Part of the National Front.' He got up and confronted the guy, and was just about to lay into him before the terrified passenger said, 'It's Sticky Little Fingers, mate! They're a band!'

'Race didn't seem to be an issue. I'm white so maybe I would say that but we just went about our young lives in and around Brixton. Leroy and I would get our pocket money nicked by bigger kids at the next-door comprehensive but that wasn't anything to do with race. If anything, I was the odd one out. It didn't seem to matter. Not to two secondary school kids, anyway.'

Martin Loveday

On a far bigger scale, just a mile from my home, things were beginning to matter and the tinder had been well and truly lit. In 1981, Brixton had its infamous riots. The outbreaks of unrest had happened on Talma Road where I lived as a baby and toddler, but to be honest, watching them unfold on the television they felt a world away from me. My road and my life were a peaceful mix of people and I was too cocooned in it to know about the hardships of the young black men and women living just around the corner from me.

'I was a bit older and out of us all, more politically aware. I had joined anti-apartheid movements aged 16 and loved talking politics with my dad. Leroy was younger and didn't engage as much back then. The uprisings – riots is the wrong word – in Brixton were the effect of so many years of problems suffered by black people and being a certain age, that was very much part of my life.'

Lynda Rosenior

For me, young and sheltered, football was on my mind and I was playing at whatever level would have me. My parents were the furthest you could get from pushy. Instead they quietly encouraged and in my house it was always about doing things that made you happy. Work hard at school, but be happy. Work hard at school? Well, I had passed my 11-plus and did okay in my O Levels but I wouldn't say I was the best scholar in south London.

'All my girls, they always had their heads in a book. All of them. All of the time. Not Leroy. He was always playing games, running, leaping. He'd leave early for school so he could play before classes began and he'd play after school. I remember one teacher at his primary school taking me and Leroy's father to one side and saying, "I'm afraid we won't make much out of Leroy." I was cross with her for that but not worried for Leroy. Boys will be boys.'

Gladys Rosenior

I played for a local club called Stockwell United and scored goals there – I once notched 12 in a 36-1 win – as well as for my school, so I got into the London side. That was a massive deal for me. I loved playing football and it felt so natural but I can't say I was one of these guys who just knew that I was going to be a professional.

'I played at Stockwell too and while Leroy was good, I'd be lying if I said he was the best player in the team. Far from it. There were a lot of really good players, explosive, but what Leroy had is desire. He would stick his head in to score a goal, and that work rate and that will to get better stood him in good stead.'

Martin Loveday

I didn't really think about it much but I guess there was a desire to become a better player. I was doing my A Levels and university might have been the option but soon, having been spotted playing for London, I was asked to trial for England schoolboys and things got that bit more serious.

Schoolboy football was a big deal back in those days. Games were shown live on terrestrial TV and attracted healthy crowds, all looking to catch a glimpse of the stars of tomorrow. I left my house for Lilleshall with my dad's calming words in my ears. 'Just go and have fun, son. Enjoy it.' And that's what I did.

Lilleshall was an amazing old building, imposing, like something out of a gothic horror novel. I though was excited and confident and just wanted to get started. Not cocky, far from it, but I never, ever walked on to a football pitch with an inferiority complex.

Trials can be strange. Many youngsters play a different game to their usual one. Plenty of talented players have looked average because they are trying too hard, trying a silly trick or simply not being themselves. I walked out there, taking in my surroundings. This was England. This was the home of the national game and here I was, Leroy, the son of a hard-working Sierra Leone couple, trying to represent his country. 'Just go out and have fun, son.'

I did. I played very well, and played my own game. I was a centre-forward, a number nine. Yes, I looked to get on the end of things but I was also there to play with my back to goal. I held things up, brought players into things, span my defender and got into the box. Nothing fancy. The basics but the basics done very well.

I was never a keen match-going fan of football as I was too busy playing. I had supported Chelsea from afar in the 1970s as I liked Peter Houseman, their exciting winger of the time who sadly later died in a car accident. I grew to like the Manchester United team of the late 1970s with players such as Gordon Hill and Steve Coppell. I loved the idea of playing alongside him.

The first game I saw live was at Crystal Palace in 1979 my brother-in-law Jimi took me and while it was again a winger who caught my eye, this time he was a black winger, Vince Hilaire, an exciting bundle of energy and skills.

No, I wasn't a massive football fan as such but I was a scholar of the game and I loved to watch other centre-forwards play. This was the early 1980s and the likes of Cyrille Regis, Paul Mariner and Joe Jordan were dominant in the British game. These guys were archetypal target men and I loved how they would not only score goals, but protect the ball, help lay the foundations for their team's attacks. That's what I wanted to do.

And I got in. An England schoolboy! What a buzz. I remember them giving me the suit that we would wear when representing the country. The trousers were Farah. Any 1980s fashion aficionado would tell you they were all the rage back then and the sharper you could get the crease, the better. Then there was the blazer. Oh my god, that navy blue blazer.

I had worn school uniforms but this was different. It felt different. Starchy. But the icing on the cake was the Three Lions badge on the top pocket. I loved wearing that blazer. My dad taught me how to properly tie a Windsor knot and there I was, all dressed and ready to play for England. If a bowler hat and an umbrella set off the archetypal Englishman's uniform then I was one too, only I had three lions and a football.

The England schoolboys set-up was first-class. I never felt intimidated or worried about my background or colour. It didn't come up. This was pure football and I loved travelling on a coach with the team, driving as far as Kilmarnock in Scotland for my debut. I remember the journey so well.

Shalamar were riding high in the album charts with *Friends*, and we played the whole thing on a loop. Here were kids from all over the country, from very different backgrounds and we're all singing along to the best in early 1980s disco. This was like dancing to 'Car Wash' with all my family and friends as a younger boy. I felt good, comfortable. *'We're gonna make it a night to remember!'* We certainly did as we beat the Scots 4-0. I scored and travelled home, feeling every bit the England player.

At that age, and after playing another game for England schoolboys, this time against Wales and scoring another goal, I was playing with such confidence. Maybe it was that blazer – that magic blazer – but I was ready to take on the world. In the autumn of 1982 I played for London Schools against a Chelsea youth team and once again, I relished the situation.

The game was played down at Richardson Evans, Wimbledon's training pitches, and I was bright all the way through, playing my way; strong, feeling stronger than anyone else there. Afterwards, I was approached by someone with a business card, saying it belonged to a Chelsea scout who had left it and that I should give the guy a call. I was of course flattered but before I could think about my next move, a smartly dressed Irishman with immaculately combed, greying hair arrived at my shoulder and told me he worked for Fulham. My life would never be the same again.

That guy was called Derry Quigley. He was Fulham's scout and he told me how impressed he was and that with the right coaching I could make it and asked if I would like to go to Fulham for a three-month trial. Chelsea and Fulham were both Second

Division clubs, down the road from each other, but here was a guy willing to stay and talk to me personally. There was no business card merely left but a real conversation.

Derry had such a soft way about him, a beautiful Irish lilt and manner, and I immediately liked him. Later I would realise he had found and influenced so many young footballers, many of them black, and I wasn't surprised. I, like others, felt comfortable, so it was Fulham for me. Yes, I'd love a trial.

Derry was soon over at my home, reassuring my parents that he would personally take me to training and back every day and that he saw real potential in me. My mum and dad were pleased but again, only if it made me happy. I was doing my A Levels at the time and it was obvious that they were going to suffer but no matter, this was a shot at seriously playing the sport I had fallen in love with.

Two months into the trial, I was taken aside by the coaches and told to go into the training ground office. Dressed in my kit, I presumed I must have done something wrong but there and then the manager Malcolm Macdonald informed me the club wanted to sign me on a short-term contract and I'd be paid £60 a week. I was a professional footballer.

* * * * *

So here I am, home. Walking into my parents' living room to tell them the big news. I had made it. Men like Malcolm Macdonald saw something in me and I was going to give football a real shot. The room was happy but calm. That summed up my childhood. Calmness and happiness. I had been protected by my family but now, I was about to go into the big bad world of football and that I would have to deal with alone.

PART TWO

LEROY

4

My Cottage, My Home

FULHAM FC. Perhaps not the most acclaimed of our capital's football clubs but to me and so many like-minded followers, the magic that shines from the place is as blinding as any floodlight over one of Spurs' many glory, glory nights, and as perfect as the feel of Arsenal's old marble halls.

Trophies and glory have never been regular or willing visitors to that famous Cottage in SW6, but there has been no shortage of wonderful footballing individuals who have opened their kit bags and brought both romance and memories to its famously Grade II-listed facade.

Johnny Haynes, that dapper playmaker of the late 1950s and early 60s, his Brylcreemed hair as perfect as his distribution. Jimmy Hill as a player, administrator, chairman and ultimately saviour who so summed up the place with his friendly enthusiasm and fervour. And it's no surprise that legends of the game came here to see out their glory days. Bobby Moore, Rodney Marsh and George Best rightly chose Fulham as the club for which to show off their talents without the pressures of the clubs they had previously represented. Even Michael Jackson found time to pop along and be immortalised in – albeit comical – statue form.

There's something about the place. The walk from Putney Bridge through the park with its old paddling pool and band stand. The red-bricked terraced houses and the ground itself. Unwilling to modernise, unapologetic for its friendliness. Neutral sections in the ground sum up Craven Cottage for this has long been a place for football lovers to stroll to and take in a game; the thing is so many simply stay.

For this young football-lover, it was the perfect club to stroll into as a starting point for my career. South-west London was where I had grown up. I was a Tooting boy but so was Citizen Smith – Robert Lindsay's character in the sitcom of the same name and he proudly wore his black and white scarf while declaring 'power to the people' on our television screens at the time.

My trial had started well. I remember Derry Quigley picking me up in his white van and driving me to Craven Cottage. As we got closer to the ground, I got more and more excited. Sure, I had played for England schoolboys in stadiums before but this was different. This could – if things went well – become my home. The place in which I ran out every other week and tried to win football matches for the men, women and kids who turned up in their thousands hoping to see me score.

We arrived and Derry introduced me to the chairman Ernie Clay, a small, bulbous man with a giant personality. Then there was the manager, Malcolm Macdonald. Or as I and every other fan of 1970s football called him – Supermac! I had grown up seeing him on *Match of the Day*. The sideburns, the swagger, the chewing gum and the goals. He had a way about him, an aura. Half Roy of the Rovers, half Mr Darcy.

He wouldn't disappoint. He was a force of nature. He took my hand, tinted glasses on, cigar in hand (that cigar was never far from reach) and enthusiastically welcomed me to the club that he was hellbent on making bigger and better, befitting of his own larger-than-life image.

Malcolm had been born and raised on one of those terraced streets adjacent to the ground. He had played under Bobby Robson and having tormented defenders in Newcastle's black and white and then Arsenal's red and white, he arrived as Fulham's charismatic manager, winning promotion to the Second Division in 1982 but ambitiously wanting so much more.

'Right, I'm driving our new centre-forward to training,' Malcolm declared, making me feel eight feet tall. 'Come with me, son.' We walked to the car park, Malcolm doing all the talking, and got into his Citroen CX. These were the new cars with the mad suspension that sunk the car to the floor. Ignition in and the car rose up (as would my anxiety levels) and off we went. Malcolm was telling me all about his plans for Fulham, about how he was going to make them a First Division club, a place they had been absent from for too long.

I though only had eyes for the digital speedometer on the dashboard. We sped past the Gillette building near Brentford, and on we went towards the training ground. Perhaps buoyed by approaching his domain, Malcolm put his foot down. His voice remained calm, but his right foot was moving to the floor. A speed of 80mph soon became 85, then 90, on to 95 and to 100. We were doing 100mph on a London road with Malcolm oblivious to my terror, enthusiastically telling me about Fulham's impending greatness. We arrived, parked up and I got out.

I walked into the dressing room, shaking. Not from the fear of meeting new team-mates but from the manager's need for speed. To be honest, meeting the squad was far from nerve-wracking. Fulham were a Second Division team and I had heard of hardly any of the players so I wasn't star-struck, I wasn't intimidated. I was shy though, and hardly the type to go in all guns blazing.

This was October time. The season was well under way and the squad had settled into the campaign. Hierarchies had been set and leaders had proverbially pissed on their territories so I wasn't going to bowl in and be the big man. That wasn't me anyway. I was naturally quiet, not painfully so but far from brash. I walked in, found my corner, got changed and politely said my hellos.

'I remember Leroy walking in, and thinking, who the fuck is this goody two shoes! He was so polite to everyone. He was the quiet type, softly spoken and just came in and got on with things. At first, I must admit, I wondered if he'd be able to hack it.'

Tony Finnegan, former Fulham team-mate

The session started and I was in my element. Wingers, forwards, defenders, crosses. Just my game. Roger Brown was the club captain and centre-half, standing 6ft 4in tall, maybe three feet wide, an ex-policeman. I'm up against him but relishing it. The cross comes in and I'm up, bang, win the header. Yes, I was quiet verbally but now I was being loud the way I knew how.

I wasn't the biggest centre-forward, just flirting with six feet. But because of that I think I had always been underestimated as a player. But I could leap. That balloon in my parents' living room had taught me that and with every cross that was swung in, there it was just dangling in the air, waiting for me to meet it. Have that!

'We had Dean Coney so it was going to be hard for Leroy and he was very raw but you immediately saw that here was a young man willing to learn. That's what stands out in my memory, this young eager striker, not the biggest, not blessed with the best touch, but so keen and if you can listen, take instructions and be eager to better yourself, you will go far.

'I liked to get my head up and play the ball in to a striker. I learnt quickly with Leroy that it was best to play it high. He wasn't so great at first with his feet so I'd knock it in to his chest or even his head and it would stick!'

Tony Gale, Fulham team-mate

Roger knew I wasn't as quiet and as shy as I made out after that session. It had been brilliant. Cross after cross for me to attack and to show off my leap with. Yes, I was raw, my movement needed work, but I had caught the eye. I had on my old Puma Kings, and I was working with professional footballers. Life was sweet.

'He might have been shy and polite but we quickly saw that here was a very good player. There was a load of good, young players at the club who had come up through the ranks from the youth team. Myself, Paul Parker and Dean Coney. Dean, what a good centre-forward he was. Dean was always seen as the next one in line but Leroy came along, could do what Dean could do but could also move. Dean would have some competition and that is never bad. Dean was a proper centre-forward. A great first touch. Left and right foot. He could hold the ball up, give it to him and the defender weren't getting it off him. Leroy though came in, perhaps without such a deft touch, but had this great mobility. Such a smooth player.'

Tony Finnegan

It might have looked strange to some as I had come into the first team squad straight from schoolboy football. I hadn't served any apprenticeship, hadn't cleaned boots or painted any stadium walls. I wasn't self-conscious of it though but maybe it annoyed some of the young guys who had done their footballing time.

'Yeah, it was an unusual route in, but Leroy did the business on the training ground. We could all see he was good. There was no jealousy. Not from me anyway. I was never jealous of anyone.'

Tony Finnegan

Two months in, I got my deal, I signed my contract and I was a Fulham player. The first thing I did with my new wage was buy my dad a bottle of whiskey and myself a wallet. Well, I'd need something to keep my new-found riches in wouldn't I? Every day I would get to the Cottage, change and enjoy the bus ride to training with the guys.

I continued to keep myself to myself but I was loving every minute of it. I was raw but so enthusiastic.

Nothing felt better than playing well. Athletes tend to call it 'The Zone'. I'm not sure about that but there were times, playing schoolboy football and at training in those early days at Fulham when I just felt at home and ready to take on anyone.

I was super fit. I could jump over a Mini! It felt so natural, running fast, turning, leaping. It all came without thought. I loved scoring goals but to be able to just sprint effortlessly, that was 'The Zone' for me. It felt normal but it felt wonderful.

It was also enough to get me a first-team debut. In early December 1982, Malcolm told me I would be his number nine at fellow promotion hopefuls Leicester City. I was ecstatic. I can't say nerves ever came into it with me. I wasn't a flash guy, but I did have an inner confidence. I knew I could play and so while I was nervous, I wasn't scared.

It turned out to be a memorable day at Filbert Street but not for any *Boy's Own* reasons. In the first half I went down under a heavy challenge and broke my collarbone. I managed to play the rest of the game (we were made of stern stuff back then) but that would be the end of my first-team input that season. You wait for opportunities and then, crack, a bone is broken and that's that for a while.

I'd get fit again but it was back to the drawing board. I was as raw as one of those chickens my mum would pluck back in Brixton. I had ability and enthusiasm but to make it as a pro, you need to – especially as a centre-forward – be cute. You need to understand how to work defenders and how to create and exploit space. For that, I needed to be coached. Luckily at Fulham, we had some of the best of those.

Ray Harford was football through and through, a northerner with thoughts about the game that were as deep as his wonderful voice. Ray was a brilliant coach. He was old-school and had that wicked sense of humour to match, but he was also very innovative. Way ahead of his time. He talked about POMO – Position Of Maximum Opportunity. Ray would drill into me how to make a run into the box. Today I watch football and it infuriates me when I see Premier League strikers not able to make the right sort of run. The game seems to have gone backwards. Ray would go mad!

Sure, he could bollock you – and when he shouted you stopped and listened – but it was never done with hatred behind his eyes. He wanted your attention and you had better give it to him because what he was about to tell you would make you a better footballer. It was that simple.

My teenage self, in those early days working with him, could be on the end of a lashing from Ray, and was less likely to be so philosophical about his reasons and technique. I remember once in training, Ray was working with the forwards on our first touch. Dean Coney (or Dixie as he was known, after Dixie Dean) had a fantastic touch. He could kill a ball with his back to goal on his chest, thigh, wherever. I was more mobile and the consensus was, my touch needed working on.

Cliffy Carr was sending diagonal crosses into the box for me to kill on the chest. In they came and off the ball went. None were sticking. People were watching and it wasn't happening for me. Ray, at first supportive, had had enough. 'Fuck off.'

'What, Ray?' I said.

'You heard.'

Had I though?

'Fuck off on the angle,' he said, with a withering tone. Five small words but my god did they sting. *Fuck off on the angle*. He had had enough and it was time for me to fuck off and watch. 'Dixie, get in here and show him how it's done.' Dean strolls in, Cliffy launches one, Dean kills it dead, spins and bang, he smashes the ball into the net. How rubbish did I feel? Here I was, a new pro, trying to get the staff thinking about me as potentially their centre-forward and I'm being told to fuck off on the angle.

Derry Quigley drove me home that day after training and it wasn't long before he grew tired of the sulking adolescent in his passenger seat.

'What is wrong with you?' he asked.

'Ray.'

'What about him?'

'He dug me out in front of everyone,' I moaned. 'Told me to fuck off on the angle.'

'So what?'

I couldn't believe Derry's words. Derry, always the shoulder to cry on, always on us young players' side, and he's having a go too.

'Ray's right,' Derry said. 'You know he's right. You're not Dixie, you're Leroy. Dixie can just push off. You need to get sideways on, you can then knock the ball into your path and whoosh, you're away. Dixie hasn't got your pace. Play to your strengths. Get sideways on, son. Don't worry, Ray and all the staff know how good you are, but they'll also make you better. If you let 'em.'

I went home, found a ball and a wall and practised and practised, banging the one against the other, and controlling the thing with either foot. In time, because I was standing sideways on, I could quickly react to where the ball was going to go. I had always been able to head the ball but now, thanks to Ray's telling off and some wise words from Derry, I was becoming a more complete striker. In football, you often need to be told to 'fuck off' to become that bit better.

That episode summed up Derry. He had never played the game professionally but he knew all there was to know about it. He could spot a young player (the list of those players he knew is like a who's who of London talent) and he knew how to tweak their games to make them better. He wouldn't put a tracksuit on – always in a suit, Derry – but with a few words, he made the game simple. I love proper football men like that who are in it because they love it. They don't promise or expect great riches or big fame, they just look, observe, advise and make you play the game of football that bit better.

Derry gave you room to be your own man. He would amble over and with his dulcet Irish tone, would offer his words of wisdom but in such a way that made you think, made you question yourself and made you want to improve. He didn't tell you what to do, he offered pearls of wisdom. It was up to you what you did with them. By making your own choices, you became a man. My dad was the same, and I loved them both for that ability.

Towards the end of the season, with my collarbone back intact, I was feeling far more part of the furniture at Fulham. I was far from out of my shell but I would arrive into training, feeling more and more part of a squad that hoped to reach the Mecca that is top-flight football.

I've mentioned the captain, Roger Brown, a leader in every sense of the word. Ray Lewington was another. Ray was in midfield and was a big part of our dressing room. Gordon Davies up front was quiet. All he cared about was scoring goals and that was it. It was admirable in many ways. I was always thinking about linking up play, bringing players into the game, the team. Not Gordon. Goals, goals, goals. We could be 3-0 down, Gordon would score in the last minute and he would run off, his arm aloft in the same way it always was, a wry grin on his face.

Then there was 'Dixie' Dean Coney, a brilliant and chirpy cockney centre-forward, Gerry Payton, or 'Bombhead' as we called him due to him having the biggest-sized head in football. Tony Finnegan was there for a bit but left shortly after I arrived. Tony was perhaps the most naturally gifted wide player around London football at the time but never clicked with the staff. Some bemoaned his attitude but that never sat right with me. If a black player is overly and obviously confident, he always had an attitude problem, as if he wasn't subservient enough, not willing to say 'yes, sir' to his elders and betters.

Paul Ince got it later on. Here was this cocky east London boy and many – including Alex Ferguson in years to come – criticised his attitude. A white guy shows the same confidence and he is simply that; confident, sure of himself, an asset to the team. Ince, brilliant at Manchester United, the self-styled Guv'nor, has a bit of an attitude problem. Eric Cantona, also brilliant at Manchester United, wears his collars up as if to say, 'Je suis le Guv'nor' and according to the world, he's brimming with self-belief.

Tony suffered for that. I'd never seen a young player so sure of himself and his ability. I believe that Malcolm once asked him, while he was in the youth team, where he was going to play. 'England,' came the confident reply, before he had even got a sniff of Malcolm's team. Now to me that is confidence that can be harnessed and utilised. Tony was released shortly afterwards. Not that he was put off, forging a good career for himself at clubs such as Crystal Palace.

Then there was Tony Gale, the life and soul of the dressing room, always upbeat, always telling jokes, always with a smile. He was a great footballer too, a brilliant passer of the ball. Not always the bravest though. I don't mean that as it sounds. It's just Tony wasn't the quickest centre-half to stick his face in where it hurts. No, his game was about starting off attacks. Reading the game was what made Tony stand out. Long balls up front to us strikers, or short, sharp passes into midfield, Tony's distribution was spot on. Anyway, he had Roger beside him to do all the dirty work.

> 'I was very vocal in the dressing room. I loved all that. I had come through when the likes of Bobby Moore were senior players. You learnt to take the stick and then give it. I met up with Paul Parker recently and after a couple of beers he admitted that he was terrified of me when he was young. I asked why and he said that it was because I was always in the thick of all the verbals, but I did it so young kids grew up, just like I had done when I started out. Leroy took the banter well and mark my words, soon he was dishing it out as well as anyone.'
>
> *Tony Gale*

They were all good guys, although I had a problem with Robert Wilson, a midfielder who I felt had a horrible attitude. He had a cutting sense of humour, always digging people out but not in any funny way. He was a decent player but lacked pace and would spend most of the game fouling people. He did have a handy knack of scoring goals from midfield though.

There were the usual nicknames. The brilliant Ray Houghton, having a Scottish accent, was of course called 'Sweaty'. Ray had arrived from West Ham and told Les Strong that he hated the name Sweaty (as in Sweaty Sock – Jock). Les took Ray into the dressing room and said, 'All right lads, I'd like to introduce you to your new team-mate, Sweaty.' That's football. Never show your weaknesses.

Paul Parker, the club's brilliant young defender, was 'Arnie' after the kid in *Diff'rent Strokes*, the popular TV programme about two black kids adopted by a rich American family. Paul didn't seem to mind.

We had a young goalkeeper from Liverpool called Ian Douglas, who we called 'Yosser'. Not that he looked like the famous character from *Boys from the Blackstuff*. The poor kid had terrible acne issues and with all those spots and puss on his face, someone shouted, 'Boys from the Blackheads.' I believe he's a top policeman, now.

I was just Leroy. I hadn't dare tell anyone that my real name was Willie. Imagine a black guy going into a football dressing room in 1983 and saying, 'Hi, I'm Willie.' He'd have been crucified. Leroy was bad enough. *Fame* was on the telly and of course, Leroy was one of the main characters. A fit, young black man, brilliant at dancing. Stereotypical of course so Leroy would do just fine as a nickname for me.

'I bet you're a good dancer ain't you, Leroy?' was often a question asked as we all prepared for a regular trip to the Hammersmith Palais. The thing was, I did love dancing, I was good at it too – still am – but back then I would shy away from it, not wanting to conform to the stereotype. 'Nah,' I'd say, my back sheepishly against the nightclub wall. *Don't give them any ammunition.*

Despite hiding my moves, I was learning to get on with things. Back from my broken collarbone I got on with life in the reserves, playing in the old Football Combination, a tough place of learning for any aspiring football scholar.

Once at Craven Cottage against Millwall, our Welsh defender Jeff Hopkins had some choice words for Mick McCarthy. Even back then, it was clear that this young centre-half was not a defender to pick on. Proper hard! Jeff, bless him, wasn't. Millwall had a corner, and I was marking Mick. We'd been having a good tussle but Jeff was still in Mick's ear.

'You know what,' Mick said with that guttural Yorkshire tone. 'You're fucking shit, you are.' He then turned to me and said,

'You though, you've got something, you have.' Sod Jeff. I felt on top of the world, hearing Mick say that. Suddenly I was back in the playground and the hardest kid at school was telling me I was good. Maybe soon, I would be back in that first team.

Off the pitch, my learning curve now extended to women and a relationship. I met Karen at Furzedown Sixth Form College in Tooting and from the off we looked the odd couple, though not because she was white. Even to the most one-eyed bigot, that would have been the last thing he noticed. Karen had this sharp, blue mohican when I met her. So, there was this punk girl from Tooting with spiky blue hair on a date and walking hand in hand with this black soul boy wearing his dad's old long 1950s tweed jacket. Not that I cared what people thought. My mixed upbringing on Thornbury Road had seen me care little for race division and when we got very strange looks, I always presumed it was because of Karen's hair, not the colour of our skin.

We were complete opposites. Our music tastes – so important to teenagers – were totally different but Karen opened my ears to other sounds. I loved my soul and disco and I remember Karen wanting to take me to see The Cure at Crystal Palace. I was very dubious but I left loving them. I still do. Soon I was getting home and putting on The Doors, Pink Floyd and other bands influenced by my new girlfriend. Not that she was as easy to turn as me. Karen was militant in her tastes and however much I played Luther Vandross and Earth, Wind & Fire, she never swayed.

With our musical tastes mixed as well as our 'cultures', Karen and I got serious and by the summer of 1983, we were living together in a local hostel, with a child on the way. Karen had got pregnant so I was now a young footballer waiting. Waiting for my first child, waiting to find a proper home and waiting to break into the first team.

And if all that wasn't worrying enough, I had my first pre-season to get used to. I immediately hated pre-season. Karen, heavily pregnant, would be kept awake most nights by her twitching boyfriend. 'No, no,' I'd be saying in my sleep. 'No, don't make me, I don't want to,' I'd moan while poor Karen lay awake next to me. Trainee therapists would argue I was showing classic signs of anxiety due to impending fatherhood. They'd be wrong. I was having nightmares about the next day's hill run.

It was hardcore. I was naturally fit, but this really was hard, designed to break your will! Dramatic, yes, but that's how I felt back then. You'd often arrive unable to walk properly from the day before but off we'd go to Richmond Park for more. There was this one circuit – Pork Chop Hill it was called – which took you past this pond and up this steep hill. Mosquitoes were everywhere under the July sun. The first time I did it, I was so eager to impress I raced off, sprinting around the park and up the hill, sprinting home and collapsing at the line.

Terry Mancini, one of the coaches and a great character, looked flabbergasted. Had he and my equally puzzled-looking team-mates not seen it done that well before? 'Leroy, you have to do it ten times, mate,' came the words that filled my lungs with terror. I was puking hard by the third time but puking was very much the norm back in those days.

I longed to work with the ball, especially with Ray Harford. Malcolm was very much a manager in a suit, a great motivator, he could make you feel like Pele before a game. Occasionally though he would strut on to the training pitch and show his class. 'Roof of the net, lads,' he'd shout at us strikers. I'd have a go and the ball was over the bar and away. 'Give it, 'ere,' he'd shout back. Malcolm would then get ten balls and nonchalantly swat each one into the roof of the net. Then his knees would give in and he'd be off. Supermac indeed!

So super was Malcolm that he didn't spend any money, building a side better than anything the locals had seen for a long time. Instead he wheeled and he sorted deals, expertly manipulating free transfers, but what he saw was the promise of youth at Fulham and those kids would get a chance.

Fulham had been brilliant throughout the 1982/83 season, heartbreakingly only dropping from the top three on the last day of the season. Needing a win at relegation-threatened Derby, we were trailing 1-0 with only minutes left. On hearing a whistle, Derby fans invaded the pitch thinking they were safe and there was no way of getting them off. The game was abandoned and despite Malcolm's calls for a replay, the Football League decided against it and top-flight football was gone for another year.

Actually it would be for nearly 20 years but all that was on my mind – going into the 1983/84 season – was securing a place in the first team. Unfortunately football's gods were as unkind to me as they had been to my club at Derby. Playing in the reserves at the beginning of the season, I landed awkwardly from a jump and my knee went. My knee. That joint that would later dog my career had its first problem and with the cartilage taken out, I wouldn't be kicking a ball for a few long months.

That injury taught me a lot, mostly about pain. I recall the plaster coming off and beads of sweat start to appear on my forehead. That was pain. Trying to stand up from my hospital bed, the plaster from my groin to my toes, and the damn thing slipping, and in doing so ripping into the scar. Just standing up took me two hours, the sweat pouring off of me. I'm ashamed to admit that I wondered what Karen had been moaning about after the birth of my eldest, Liam.

Once my ordeal was done, the hospital staff asked me to help a ten-year-old girl – a ballet dancer – who was refusing to try and get up from her bed. I sat with her for hours, reassuring her, but deep down dreading the pain she was about to experience.

I was soon back in the weights room at Fulham, working on my quads and building up my strength. Fulham drew Liverpool in the League Cup that autumn. Liverpool would go on to become

European champions that season so taking them to two replays was quite a coup for a team struggling to match the previous campaign's form.

I'm not a patient man but here I was having to be. I had tasted first-team action but only the smallest of bites and this was a very good side, one that wouldn't be easy to break in to. Those three Liverpool games proved that. I'd have to learn, wait and learn some more.

I watched studiously from the sidelines and while Ian Rush and Kenny Dalglish were the cream of the crop, I found my eyes wandering to Alan Hansen and Mark Lawrenson. I liked to study centre-halves, see how they moved, how they might be exploited. I had to be stronger and willing to take the blows when I jumped. I had done it with our own Roger Brown and now I was looking at the country's best, hoping, no, fantasising about one day playing at Craven Cottage.

It was Christmas – Boxing Day – that that fantasy became reality. I had worked hard, the knee was strong again and with Derby the visitors, Malcolm picked me and with the number nine on my back, I ran from the famous cottage for my home debut.

It had been over a year since my debut at Leicester but here I was, finally back playing – and scoring. A tap-in and a header, both at the Hammersmith End. Two goals on my home debut and then the chant came down from that famous mass (the crowd was just under 8,000) of Fulham fans. 'Leroy! Leroy! Leroy!' They were chanting my name. There were 8,000 fans in the ground but for that moment, when I first heard my name, I could have been playing to a packed Maracana in Rio.

There was a lot to deal with. Racist slurs from opponents and fans alike temporarily took their toll but I had learned to deal with it. I had found an inner strength necessary to make it in the tough word of football. The overriding thing was that I loved playing in front of the Fulham fans. They had this homely manner about them. Don't get me wrong, they were as fanatical as any others around – the small hardcore perhaps even more so considering they had for years travelled the country watching some poor teams and results – but they summed up the club with their friendly ways. You felt you knew them personally and that made you try even harder for the cause.

I'd be lying if I said it was only goals that drove me on. I wasn't like Gordon Davies in that sense. I was their number nine but the fans liked me because they saw what playing in front of them meant to me. I gave everything to the team but scoring goals was only part of my job.

As I played more over the next season and a half, the art of the centre-forward became more and more important to me. I wanted to hold that ball up, work central defenders and create space for team-mates. Maybe I could have been more single-minded or even greedy but that wasn't my game. I scored goals, not prolifically, but my overall graft made me a crowd favourite. *Leroy! Leroy! Leroy!*

The old Second Division – as the Championship is today – was a hard place to learn your trade; 42 games, up and down the country against hard men when they were hard. Sorry to sound like an old pro, belittling the state of the modern game, but when you are trying to get the better of defenders such as Sam Allardyce, you had better be ready for more than a mere tussle.

I remember one game at Huddersfield. Jeff Hopkins was a lovely guy but was prone to getting into trouble on a football pitch. He might mis-control the ball and was always so eager to win it back for his team, so focused that often, fouls occurred.

On this occasion, Jeff, the ball bouncing away from him, lunged to win it and *crack*, he had broken the leg of his opponent. It's a horrible sound that crack. Players dread hearing it, but there it was, filling the Yorkshire air, and boiling the blood of the victim's team-mates. Cue mayhem, an immediate red card, no arguments and Jeff, looking ashen-faced, holding up his hands as Huddersfield players surrounded him with genuine hate in their eyes.

Playing for the Terriers that day was Sam Allardyce and he wanted retribution. Fists clenched, he was screaming at Jeff, following him from the pitch, being held back by the coaching staff, telling Jeff exactly what he wanted to do with him. Fifteen minutes later I came off injured and found a distraught Jeff in the dressing room, in tears, inconsolable about what he had done. I was explaining to him that he wasn't malicious and that accidents happen in football and suddenly a fist came flying through the door. Through the door! It was as if the Incredible Hulk had arrived at Bloomfield Road. It wasn't, it was Sam Allardyce, though he was just as angry and just as scary.

I scrambled Jeff into the showers as stewards dealt with the mass of muscle and malice that is Sam Allardyce. Out on the pitch, we had another player sent off and eventually left the ground with police escorts.

That was life in mid-1980s second-tier football. And I loved it. Soon though, and without any planning on my part, phone calls would be made, decisions would be taken, and I would become a First Division footballer.

5

Dodging Bullets

IN April 1968, Enoch Powell, MP for Wolverhampton South West, stood before a Conservative Association meeting in Birmingham and delivered his 'Rivers of Blood' speech. In it he lamented the rising number of Commonwealth immigrants arriving on these shores, of how 'Negros' had taken over the streets of Wolverhampton and how Sikh communities were forcing their 'inappropriate' customs upon good old British values.

The river of blood line was of course the showstopper but there is another passage that also strikes a chord. Powell spoke of a recent meeting he had had with 'an ordinary working man'. Having discussed the weather (one of those great British customs under threat) the man said to Powell, 'If I had the money to go, I wouldn't stay in this country.' Powell quipped that the then Labour government would soon be gone, but it wasn't party politics that was making the man so irate.

'I have three children,' he told Powell. 'All of them have been through grammar school and two of them are married now, with family. I shan't be satisfied 'til I have seen them all settled overseas. In this country in 15 or 20 years' time the black man will have the whip hand over the white man.'

It was a bold statement and I wonder if that irate 'ordinary white man' was in England in the early 1980s – 15 years after his chat with Enoch Powell. For then, when I was entering my chosen profession, the black man was far from having any whip over any white man.

In the days and months after my run in with two racist opponents I'd had many thoughts and inner arguments about where to go next. I had felt disarmed by their words, not ready to fight. A whip hand to the white man? Do me a favour. I had nothing (or I thought I had nothing) and that had left me wondering where I go next.

A voice in my head wondered if it was worth going on. I loved playing football and all I wanted to do was play in front of big, adoring crowds and help teams win games by scoring goals. It's what I had done all my young life, but suddenly the professional game had shown itself to be a darker, scarier place and I simply wasn't prepared. Could I carry on?

'I'm not surprised Leroy found the racial verbals hard as he hadn't come through football's system. To play schoolboy football with London and England is great but it ain't our football. It's all polite.

"If you play youth team football and have worked as an apprentice you get very used to the game's ways and its language. I had been around clubs and football men, old-school men and I had heard it all. I had been an apprentice, and even at youth level at clubs you'd get all that. "You black this, you nigger that."

'I was in the system. I heard the nigger shouts, I heard the monkey chants. Even in training if you beat a team-mate you'd get it back then, "You cheeky black cunt." It affected me at first. Like it did Leroy. I wouldn't get showered. I'd sit there all shy and not want to talk to anyone but by the time I played first-team football, I was hardened. Ready.

'Youth team football was very competitive and so many of those kids didn't have the minerals to carry on. I could cite loads of kids who had all the talent in the world but fell away. It was really hard. You could get walked all over. As an apprentice you had to have inner steel and take pride in what you did. I had to get Kenny Sansom's boots spotless at Palace and I took pride in that job. You'd get shouted at and some would walk away in tears. Leroy never had that so I am sure coming in and getting it verbally from players was hard.

'It was graft. Running up the terraces in the summer, doing work around the clubs, getting shouted at. You had to harden up and you had to be strong otherwise you'd just be another kid who never made it. There were so many young, black footballers who dropped out. I'm not saying they were all put off by racism but there was an extra mental strength us black kids had to have. For Leroy, he got it suddenly and at the highest level.'

Tony Finnegan

My dad and I talked about what had happened and how I should deal with it. Calmly – always calmly – he recounted his time in a court of law, having being attacked by these irate Teddy Boys, of how he had listened to the patronising questioning of pompous barristers, how he had taken their arrogant jibes before letting them know just how educated he in fact was. He said to me that my talent would have the same effect. Take the abuse, use it to your advantage and show them just how good you are and how wrong they are.

The key was not to let these people, be they in the crowd or on the pitch, get under my skin. Dad always used humour to combat hatred and I could do the same. I had the talent so why not use the wit? Blow them a kiss, give them a wink, raise an eyebrow, score a goal. Armour! Now I had armoury and I would never allow mere words to get to me again.

> 'Leroy's upbringing meant he dealt with it differently too. He had strong family support, a good home, a father figure, something I never had. He is also west African. I'm Jamaican and they are poles apart in terms of temperament. I also have a bit of Irish in me from my dad's side, put that together and I ain't having it, you know what I mean?'
>
> *Tony Finnegan*

Emboldened, I was now aware that my chosen profession was not going to be the most welcoming. Enoch Powell was no longer a viable political voice but the many cities around the United Kingdom had become fertile ground for far right factions such as the National Front and later Combat 18. Both would use football as nurseries from which to expand their membership, soap boxes from which to preach and makeshift battlegrounds on which to flex their violent muscle.

> 'I was aware that Leroy and Paul Parker and other players got it from both players and fans regularly. It is hard looking back. Obviously, it never happened to me and in my mind there is no colour in football, just us players but because I was never on the end of it, I can easily just say "ignore it, play the game, shut them up by scoring goals". Easier said than done. What I do know is, players such as Leroy and those before him paved the way and have made sure that the problems are nowhere near like they were back then.'
>
> *Tony Gale*

Despite an ugly backdrop, progress had been made with Viv Anderson. In 1978, the elegant Nottingham Forest full-back made his England debut and in doing so became the first black man to play for the national team.

I remember that so well. First of all there was the kit, England's Admiral strip, with the red and blue stripes along the arms. It was made from the worst sort of itchy nylon but I had it and I loved it. And here was a black man wearing it and walking from Wembley's old tunnel to represent his country.

I'm sure Viv didn't comprehend just how symbolic that moment was, as he was righty focused on just playing and playing well but to young men like me, he was changing the world. He looked so cool too. As Viv stepped out on to the Wembley turf, Michael Jackson was in Los Angeles recording his album, *Off The Wall*. The cover had Michael in a tuxedo with his tight afro. So iconic.

To me, Viv had all that. There he was with his long legs, the tight afro, making tackles, starting attacks. I watched later that night with my England top on and felt an amazing sense of pride. For me and even for others who had no interest in playing football, here was a modest guy proving to us that in the United Kingdom we could achieve whatever we wanted to.

Pride, though, soon turned to fear. As the game wore on, I hoped Viv wouldn't make a mistake, especially one that might lead to a goal. Back then whenever you watched the news or opened a newspaper, you dreaded reports of the black rapist or the black mugger. Their arrest photos would fill the pages or the television screens and you could almost hear a collective nationwide gasp, one that almost screamed, 'We told you so!'

With England I feared Viv having a shocker. Not that I didn't appreciate just how brilliant a player he was, but one little mistake would have been highlighted, scrutinised and used as an excuse to not pick any more black players. See, *they're not up to it*.

I would often watch England and think like that. John Barnes was later so often the scapegoat for England despite being one of the most gifted players to ever play for this country. When he was good, he was among England's finest, but when he was bad he was Jamaican-born and his heart wasn't in it.

The different approaches made by the country to him and Chris Waddle always fascinated me. Both were majestic wingers in the same England set-up, both had an abundance of skills, and both could be described as languid in the way they sometimes moved. Chris was brilliantly laid-back, John was too laid-back. A Caribbean man taking it too easy.

That was football, that was its attitude. Preconceptions of players – black players – followed them around, mainly without being contested. Instead it was up to the black player – just to get anywhere near an even keel with his white peers – to be brilliant. Brilliance alone could perhaps change attitudes. No pressure then.

One group of players up for that challenge were West Bromwich Albion's three black stars, Brendon Batson, Laurie Cunningham and Cyrille Regis. For one black player to break through at a club and shine was a reason for celebration, for three in the same team to shine and contribute to a brilliant team dynamic, this was unheard of. It changed so much.

They were all fantastic. Laurie was slick, full of tricks, ridiculously cool in everything he did. Cyrille was a hero of mine. A centre-forward's centre-forward; all hustle, bustle and muscle with an amazing physique matched by a steely and determined mind. Racial barriers (like central defenders) were there to be knocked down and he was the man to do it.

Then there was Brendon. Perhaps not as lauded as the other two but what a difference he made, both on and off the pitch. Being a black footballer back in the 1970s and 80s often felt a bit like the slave trade. That's a bold statement and I don't mean it flippantly but players felt like they were being examined by the white establishment.

Take off your clothes, stand in the middle of the room. Your thighs manhandled, *look at that power*. Your physique admired, your power craved, your backside tapped. *This kid looks perfect. Let's hope his attitude is.* Of course this didn't literally happen but there was this sense that we could be moulded into something to suit our owners.

Brendon was interesting because that something was usually a skilful winger or bombastic striker. Black players at the time weren't supposed to be tactically astute, they weren't supposed to put in a shift or even enjoy a game on a cold night somewhere not so nice. Black players were two-dimensional weren't they?

Brendon was a full-back, like Viv Anderson, and he played in the same manner in which he now administrates. Methodically, studiously and calmly. He could tackle, pass, head the ball, all the things that any good defender should be able to do, and he did them brilliantly.

Their manager, Ron Atkinson, would famously call them The Three Degrees, after the famous and incredibly successful female vocal group at the time. In some quarters, and more so later, it was scoffed at as an all too easy comment.

'It was just a throwaway line from Ron. The group had a gig at Birmingham's Big Night Out and came to the Hawthorns to do some promotional stuff and Ron said, "We've got our own Three Degrees." The press loved it but it wasn't anything major.

'We were radical you see. That label stuck because we were so radical. To have three black players in a team just wasn't seen.

'I'm now an agent and when I tell young black players that in 1977 there was only four black guys in the top flight, they don't believe me. It was radical and so it stuck. Typical Big Ron really, it got us headlines and exposure.'

Cyrille Regis

I remember hearing that they had been called The Three Degrees and loved it. While some went on about it being lazy from Atkinson, I felt it was helpful. Here was a black group that every Sunday night were on our televisions live from the Palladium. Here was a success story, having hit after hit and now the three footballers who had been given their same name, were proving themselves a similar positive success in the white-dominated world of football.

Not that positives were in abundance in England's football stadiums in the mid-1980s. I remember going to play at Leeds for Fulham in 1984. Elland Road might not have welcomed the sort of success that it had enjoyed in the 1960s and 1970s but it remained one of the most impassioned stadiums in the country.

Playing there is never dull and on this occasion, the locals were in particularly boisterous mood. We got a throw-in down at the big Kop end that housed the fanatical home support. Paul Parker and I were closest and looked to get our attack back on track. As we got to the corner flag any thought of launching that attack went from our minds as we were met in the corner by thousands of fans with hate in their eyes, intent on unsettling these two young black footballers who had dared to come to their town to play a game of football.

Usually there were the monkey chants, the 'ooh-ooh-ooh' noises that all black players had been subject to at the time. There were the chants about shooting niggers and the bananas that fell from the terraces of 1980s football stadia – local greengrocers of that era owe us black footballers a fortune if you ask me – with increasing regularity. What happened was none of the above.

Instead, Paul and I were greeted with 5,000 or more Leeds fans with their right hands, erect to the sky, shouting 'Sieg Heil' as if not attending a Second Division football match on a rainy Yorkshire afternoon but a 1930s Nuremberg rally. Paul and I looked at each other in disbelief. Maybe, despite being young, we had already become accustomed to the usual chants about our colour but this was something harder, something more political.

In 1976, David Bowie – another Brixton boy! – had returned to England and (presumably satirically) given the Nazi salute before exulting the virtues of Adolf Hitler. His supporters probably correctly argued that here was a showman who was playing to packed-out stadiums and with his own rock panache was ironically underlining just how easily the masses could be led. That day, in that hate-filled corner of Elland Road, the masses were not being ironic and they certainly weren't being satirical. Hatred was in their eyes, it was in their hearts and it showed just how deep the far right had sunk their dirty nails into the national game.

At least I could get some respite from such hatred every other week. Craven Cottage was an oasis away from the vicious chants. That's why I had such sympathy for Paul Canoville at Chelsea. Paul would take the same sort of abuse that we all took away from home but then he would play at Stamford Bridge and so often he would hear the same things from some of his own supporters. I say supporters but Chelsea had fallen victim to National Front and Combat 18 groups who would leaflet the ground trying to recruit and for Canoville, life got that bit harder.

We are all individuals and we had to deal with the racism that came our way regularly in our own different ways. Paul Parker and I were shaken by what happened at Leeds, but it wasn't spoken about in the dressing room. That wasn't football's way. It came at a time when I was doubting my place in the game after after being so harshly abused and I had to deal with it internally.

You didn't want to be seen as the victim. Had you gone to the manager or even to your team-mates you might be seen as a troublemaker, someone not focused on the team. *It's only banter*. Well, okay, if it's only banter then give it back.

> 'I had played non-league football which had hardened me physically but soon learnt in the pro game that I would have to deal with racism too. My attitude was if you wind me up, you will get a more determined and better player.
>
> 'There was loads of verbals but I was in control of my actions. I had an inner confidence, bordering on arrogance. If you abuse me, I am quicker than you, I'm faster than you and my team-mates are brilliant so all I am going to do is pull my socks up, throw a few elbows and put the ball in the back of the net.
>
> 'It made you angry but back in the 1970s you had to choose to use it as motivation because if you were going to let it get to you and make you anxious or worried, you simply weren't going to be a professional footballer.'
>
> ### *Cyrille Regis*

After it happened to me, I thought about how abusive opponents would pat themselves on the back, smugly chatting about a job well done, on how they had mugged off a young striker and even somehow weakened me. Like Cyrille I was adamant that I would pull my socks up, take the abuse on the chin and let the football do the talking. It was the only way.

> 'I was young and angry and weren't having it. At Palace, Andy Gray was a bit addicted to the slot machines and we used to go to the Brixton Snooker Club after training. The thing is we didn't realise that everyone in there was Millwall. One day, the week of a game at The Den –

the old Den! – a letter gets sent to the training ground, addressed to me and Andy. We open it and it says, "If you step out on to that pitch on Saturday, you're both dead. We'll catch up with you in Brixton and you're dead." Well, Jimmy Cannon showed it around to the coaches and they are all laughing. To them it's banter. They're all cracking up like children. So it's funny to them. It's a fucking death threat to us!

'On matchday, we pack our kit bags and in it I'm putting in a machete-like thing from my mum's kitchen, and Andy has a big knife. You never know. We were expecting an ambush. Looking back what are they going to do? We got off the coach and we're in the dressing room. It's all bravado but they were scary days. I would have used it, I promise you!

'I remember this skinhead in the crowd giving me so much stick. "You black cunt!" he's screaming.

'"Black cunt? Look at your bird. She can't stop looking at me!" I said. Oh he went mad, while I'm laughing.

'"I'm going to kill you!" he screamed. Brilliant. Back then you could have it with them. Today the linesman would be flagging and you'd be off.'

Tony Finnegan

I'm not sure what our white team-mates at the time made of the things they must have heard being said from the stands and from opponents alike. As I say, it was never really talked about. To them perhaps it was the same as stick that everyone got. A red-haired player was 'a ginger cunt', a larger player was 'a fat cunt', and so on and so forth.

'You'd hear that. You'd hear people saying that all sorts of people get abuse. But when it's about your skin, it's different to being ginger or fat. That argument doesn't stand up I'm afraid.

'Discrimination because of the colour of your skin has historical connotations as for centuries people felt superior to other people due only to the colour of their skin. The slave trade was based on such prejudices and so to suggest that redheads or overweight people have suffered the same is factually incorrect.'

Cyrille Regis

Henry VIII! England had a red haired, overweight king once. Maybe one day when there is a black king, we can talk. Team-mates seemed oblivious to how we felt but as I say, the team and the result was the most important thing and of course, that's what I was focused on too, it's just that I had to try to win a game of football in often far harsher circumstances.

One Saturday we went to Portsmouth. We were walking from the pitch and I caught the eye of a boy, no older than ten, who was behind the fences. He was accompanied by an adult whom I presumed to be his father. As I got closer and walked past the fans, the boy spat at me, covering my red (actually it was pink as it had faded in the wash – money was tight at the time) Fulham away shirt with phlegm. I stopped in amazement. I couldn't believe what this kid had done.

I said nothing. I was speechless and as I stood there, the adult with the boy began to laugh, then another fan laughed and then another until a group of human adults were all laughing because a child had spat at another human adult.

I froze in disbelief but my team-mate John Reeves, who was close by and had seen the incident, started to berate the fans, telling them what he thought of the kid and them. John's intentions were good but back in the dressing room when he asked if I was all right, I lost my rag.

'What about last week, John?' I asked. 'What about last week when I was getting called a black cunt? How come you didn't ask if I was all right then?' John looked shocked as did my other team-mates but I had a point to make. 'What about when the banana was thrown, what about the Nazi salutes, how come you didn't support me then?'

My point was that because the spitting incident had happened right in front of a team-mate, because it was visible and he had seen it directly, because it was isolated and based around just a few fans, he had reacted. The things that happened every week around our football stadiums were ignored by everyone. Out of sight, out of mind.

Not that it was only the country's football stadiums. Karen and I now had Liam and as we walked London's supposedly multicultural streets, some people – black and white – would cross the road so as not to see this black man, his white wife and their brown child. Karen would tell me about the abuse she would get when walking to the shops with Liam from people objecting to the colour of her son.

On our television screens, comedy shows such as *Love Thy Neighbour* and *Mind Your Language* laughed and poked fun at the otherness of non-whites living in England. *The Comedians* was hugely popular and had stand-ups telling gag after gag. I remember Charlie Williams, a black comedian (and former footballer) from the north-west who would tell all sorts of jokes about black people. I'm all for humour and laughing at the ridiculousness of our world, but when these programmes made white people feel it was okay to mock black people for having rubber lips and velcro hair, then it takes a nastier turn. Laugh it off? It's not that easy when people are judging you by how you look before they have even met you.

After Viv Anderson had made his debut for England in 1978 he was followed firstly by Laurie Cunningham and then, in 1982, by

Cyrille Regis. Cyrille's inclusion for me was huge. A big, bustling, determined number nine, he was everything I hoped to be and he did it all with a swagger that belied the abuse he received from racist fans.

Famously prior to making his England debut, he received a bullet in the post and a letter that read, 'YOU'LL GET ONE OF THESE THROUGH YOUR KNEE IF YOU STEP ON OUR WEMBLEY TURF.'

To think that some sad and lonely individual went to the bother of doing this should invite our pity but it screamed of the way many racist young men felt threatened by change. This was an act of fear from a man somehow taught along the way to be fearful of the likes of Cyrille. Big, powerful, confident, black and ready to turn white England upside down.

'The letter with the bullet came to West Brom's training ground and we had a good laugh about it. I wasn't intimidated at all. Why should I be? We all used to get loads of hate mail, especially Laurie because he had a white girlfriend.

'The guy who sent it was a coward, simple as that. Back then, if I had been getting abuse while out in London or Birmingham that would have been hard. If I had been getting beaten up or having my windows put in or my kids were abused, now, that would have been different.

'That never happened though. No one ever fronted up to me, ever. It all happened from a crowd, with that crowd mentality, or in envelopes. No one ever tried it on one-on-one. They wouldn't dare! It was confined to the stadium and because we had armour to deal with it – our talent – then bring it on.'

Cyrille Regis

Cyrille was never going to be put off by such hate, and by playing for England he was challenging it. By playing he was helping change the world.

> 'We inspired the second and third generations. We early players were just the tip of the iceberg. That's why we are still talked about and written about. What stopped racism in my mind was that more and more teams soon had black players. If you have one in your side, it's hard to racially abuse the opposition's black players. That was a big factor, more and more black players getting into football.'
>
> **Cyrille Regis**

Cyrille, Laurie, Viv, Brendon; these guys paved the way for players such as myself but racism wasn't going away any time soon. Instead, we learnt to deal with it and to cope with it. 'Ignore it, Leroy, it will go away.' I heard that a lot in my formative years as a professional footballer and to some degree that's what I did. The thing is, if you ignore it, it doesn't go away. If you ignore that sort of hatred, it cultivates it and it gets worse.

When hateful views aren't challenged they fester and they grow. Hatred must be challenged. That boy at Portsmouth's Fratton Park didn't spit on white players and he wasn't born thinking it was okay to do it to black people. That boy had been taught to hate, as had the guy who sent Cyrille Regis a bullet.

As my career progressed I began to realise the pressure black players were under not only to prove themselves worthy of even being there but also in the way we behaved. I remember in my QPR days, we played Wimbledon and I had a clash with John Fashanu. My elbow went up and I cut John, who reacted very angrily. John was big and tough but it was known within the game that he hated the sight of blood and he wasn't happy, even having to leave the pitch.

After the game, in the players' lounge, John came for me, wanting to fight there and then. He may be a martial arts expert but I was sick of his moaning and wasn't going to back down. As we went to start an ugly bar brawl, Wimbledon's Roger Joseph, a mate and fellow black player, stepped in and stopped us. As I left the ground I was ashamed. The lounge had been busy after the game and here were three black guys (Roger of course was only doing the right thing) living up to too many preconceived notions, however wrong those notions might be.

So there were added pressures as I made my way and as a young footballer, I felt quite powerless to challenge the subject of hate within the game. I guess simply by playing every week, showing them I wasn't inferior and I certainly wasn't different to a white player, that would have to do. When I sat and thought of how those two players used their words against me, of those Leeds fans, of the kid at Portsmouth, I knew though that I couldn't simply forget it and let it go. One day, when I hung up my boots, I would challenge them further.

6

Plastic Dreams

I N the early spring of 1984, Malcolm Macdonald left Fulham. My first manager was off – nothing unusual there, you get used to it – but in mysterious circumstances. Results had never reached the level of the 1982/83 campaign but under Malcolm, the club had prospered and to me anyway he was the perfect manager for young players, and Fulham had a lot of them. Malcolm was enthusiasm personified. 'You're brilliant,' he'd say. 'You're going to be a superstar.' You would leave his company ready to take on the world's greatest defenders. One day though, we walked into training and he'd gone. That's football.

Malcolm's problems seemed to stem from matters off the field. It came out that he and the chairman, Ernie Clay, hadn't seen eye to eye. Malcolm had done brilliantly on a shoestring but at the end of 1982/83, when we'd been losing 1-0 at Derby in the final game only for a pitch invasion to see it abandoned, a rift had started to form. Malcolm had pushed hard for a replay but felt that Ernie was less enthusiastic for the club to push on.

We beat Manchester City 5-1 in March 1984 at the Cottage. I scored in a good display but after the match, it was revealed that the manager's marriage was ending. Malcolm had met another woman and within weeks the tabloids had got hold of the story (according to Malcolm's autobiography, he had his suspicions that the tip-off had come from Ernie Clay himself) and soon, the scandal became too much.

I was very sad to see Malcolm go. As I've mentioned, he was by no means a hands-on coach but he filled the club like a whirlwind of positivity. The cigars and the chewing gum, the fast driving, Supermac never did things by half. He also gave me my senior debut and I don't think any footballer ever forgets the guy who does that. Now though it was a case of getting on with things.

That would be easy as Ray Harford got the job, his first as a manager, and it was a good choice. The players had so much time for Ray and his methods. It seemed seamless. The squad was full of experienced players with big personalities, and so that change went unnoticed really. No big fuss, just business as usual.

The fans were great too. They'd loved Malcolm but were never going to be impatient with Ray. He could get on with things, learn about management without the added politics from players or supporters that so often can blight a new boss.

Players like Tony Gale, Roger Brown, Ray Lewington, they were all such big characters who could look after a dressing room on their own and the respect they all had for Ray meant that life couldn't be easier for the new man. We weren't firing on all cylinders in the league – we were very much a mid-table side – but even that meant Ray could just take over and keep the wheels turning.

I was still very raw. Niggly injury problems continued throughout much of the 1984/85 season but I still scored seven goals in ten appearances and must have been noticed in the higher echelons of the game. Not that I knew or for that matter at that time in my life, cared.

I did the usual pre-season hell with Fulham not thinking about my immediate future. I was 21 and more than happy learning my trade from Ray and his staff, but in September 1985, just weeks into the season and straight out of the blue, the club came to me to say that Queens Park Rangers had made them an offer and with it being a healthy £100,000, they had chosen to accept.

Many things went through my mind on hearing the news. It was another London club, based near Fulham so no upheaval for Karen and Liam there. It was a First Division club, the top flight, a big step up and that was of course very appealing. It was a challenge I felt more than ready for. It was hard though to contemplate leaving Fulham. They had been my footballing family, guiding me through this mad career choice of mine and everyone from the players, staff and fans would be hard to leave.

But football isn't anything like family. The club had their own interests at heart. They had cashflow concerns and a six-figure sum for a young striker was too tempting. They also had Dean Coney, a talented young striker, and if we're comparing football to families then I was the brother being asked to go. So I went home to Karen, told her I was leaving the club that had always been my employer but that she wouldn't have to pack any bags and we got on with our lives. There would though, of course, be lots of new things I would have to get used to.

Queens Park Rangers had been an exciting club in the early 1980s. Under the stewardship of Terry Venables they had caught the eye when winning the Second Division in 1983, the season Fulham had so cruelly been denied promotion in the last game. I had watched them that year and been impressed with a fine side, a side that had also reached the FA Cup Final the year before, losing out to Tottenham, but only after a replay.

They had finished a brilliant fifth in the First Division in 1983/84, prompting Barcelona to swoop, making Terry 'El Tel'. Replacing Shepherd's Bush for Las Ramblas clearly suited Venables but under new manager Alan Mullery and then Frank Sibley, Rangers struggled, avoiding the drop by just one point the following campaign. Frank would be replaced and Jim Smith – 'The Bald Eagle' as he was affectionately known within the game – who had done such a good job guiding Oxford United up the leagues, was brought in. It was Jim who bought me.

I met Jim and his chairman, Jim Gregory, a former second-hand car salesman who had done a lot to build a modern club. The days of international billionaires owning clubs and employing vastly qualified chief executives was a long way off. This was the time of local businessmen owning clubs wearing fur coats and driving gold-plated Bentleys. Meet one, you met them all.

Jim, no shrinking violet himself, sold the club and himself to me with his charm and passion for the job and the place. He pointed out the great players he had (many of them internationals) and despite their recent struggles, he vehemently believed he could win silverware. They had the players, a good fan base, a passionate, successful manager and now they had me. Their most dangerous weapon though was their pitch. Their *plastic* pitch.

On signing for QPR, I hadn't really factored in the playing surface. If I had, I honestly think I would have turned down the move. I hated that plastic pitch with a passion. There was no doubt that it was a potent advantage for the team as so many opponents hated it as much as I did, but I could never enjoy playing on it. The bounce, the toil it took on your joints. Plastic means fake and to me every game we played on it, was just that.

As well as the synthetic surface, I would have to also get used to new team-mates, something every player has to do after a move but it is a factor that can make or break a footballer's spell at any club, and with my new colleagues I'd be lying if I said I fully integrated. They were all nicer than the pitch, but like the plastic carpet, I never fully settled with them. Don't get me wrong, they weren't a nasty bunch of lads, it was just we never fully clicked.

There were plenty of big characters: Alan McDonald, Macca, the chain-smoking Northern Ireland centre-half with the strongest Ulster accent you ever heard; Steve Wicks, another centre-half, a good player but I sometimes felt he was simply too good looking to be a stalwart in defence.

Up front they had distinguished and settled strikers in Gary Bannister – a quick and decent finisher – and John Byrne – a clever number ten. John was the friendlier of the two towards me, Gary a little detached. They also had Michael Robinson, who had come for big money from Liverpool but Michael played on the right side of the attack. A good, strong runner, Michael was very funny and I'm not surprised he went on to have such a good career in the Spanish media.

I remember him always fussing about the music being played around the club. 'You and your soul music,' he'd say to me. 'It all sounds the same. Every other line is, "Yeah, yeah, yeah".'

'Put your fucking music on then,' I told him. So he did. The Beatles (his time up in Liverpool obviously had an effect) and the second song was 'She Loves You'. The chorus came on and Michael didn't even notice the words, 'She loves you, yeah, yeah, yeah.' Strange. I liked Michael though.

Martin Allen was there too. Mad Dog as he was known. Martin was in midfield, not a hard player but a hard worker. He was a bit loopy even then and the crowd loved him for it and I was always impressed that he forged out a career because he wasn't the most talented of players but he grafted. His cousins, Clive Allen and Bradley Allen, were gifted footballers but Martin had to work at it and that he did.

Running the whole show was the captain, Terry Fenwick. A good defender and brilliant organiser, he ran the club and Jim actively encouraged it. I'm not suggesting that he had Jim's ear or in any way influenced team selection but I just sensed that this was Terry's domain and if anything new was to happen, he would have to okay it. I was never close to Terry, perhaps not giving myself over fully enough to the club, his club. I did respect him though, and he rightly won England caps and was soon to follow Terry Venables to Spurs.

When I first arrived, we went out to warm up before a game at Loftus Road and being so close to the fans there, Terry introduced their new signing to a section of supporters. 'Call him Sidney,' he kept saying. 'His nickname is Sidney.' I only later realised that Terry was referring to the American actor Sidney Poitier. I must admit the comparison made me anxious.

I have said earlier that I was all for Ron Atkinson's Three Degrees comparison at West Brom, but I couldn't get on board with my new nickname at my new club. Sure, Poitier was a brilliant actor, a pioneer, a good-looking man and a huge hero of my own father's but it seemed too easy, a bit odd. I was new, I was black, I wasn't three players. No need.

Now I know that Laurie Cunningham, Brendon Batson and Cyrille Regis would not have been named the Three Degrees had they been white but being alone, the only black player at the club at the time, I took the reference in a negative way. It wasn't a great start but perhaps it was a better nickname than the one given to me by Alan McDonald after a post-match shower together.

There we were, lathered up with soap, small-talking about the game and suddenly Alan screams. 'What the fuck is that?' he says, pointing down at my nether regions.

'What do you mean, what is that, Macca?' I said, confused. 'Have you never seen one before?'

'Course I have,' Macca said. 'I've never seen one that bends like yours to the right. What do you do, fuck around corners?'

From then on, to Macca, I was called 'Sidewinder'. At least they didn't combine the two. Imagine being known as Sidney Sidewinder!

Macca was himself no stranger to stereotypical comparisons. Blessed with the strongest of accents, and with this being the mid-1980s and terrorism never far from our newspapers and TV screens, Macca had to put up with all sorts. IRA this and IRA that. I'm not sure if anyone ever bothered to find out if he was Protestant or Catholic though. *It's only banter.*

My debut at Loftus Road was an awkward and double-edged affair. I was getting used to the new surface (in other words, I was crap) but I managed to score and we won. I came off the pitch feeling pretty good about things. I hadn't played well but the fans love goals and I was off the mark.

I showered, changed and went up to the players' lounge to be greeted by a few guys up there wanting my autograph. So far, so good. I bowled over to my parents and my sisters, feeling every bit the First Division footballer, but instead of proud grins, there were only awkward silences. 'What's wrong?' I asked, feeling a bit annoyed that my family weren't sharing the rest of the room's admiration.

'We want to go home,' they said, and off they went. I couldn't understand it. Why the rush to get away and why the long faces? I had a drink with the guys and headed back to my parents' house where I found my sisters and made a beeline toward them wanting to get to the bottom of what had just happened.

'During the game that guy who asked for your autograph in the players' lounge, he didn't stop abusing you,' they told me, tears in their eyes. 'Racially abusing you. "Effing hell [none of my sisters would ever swear, not even when repeating the ramblings of a sad racist], Rosenior, you black c.u.n.t." "You're effing useless," and, "Effing hell, we've signed a useless black so and so here."' My family had been the only black faces in that part of the ground and, not used to the football stadia of the time, were understandably intimidated.

I was used to the language but what struck me was the two-faced nature of this guy. I played badly – I admit that – and I get his vitriol, but then I score and we win and he wants my autograph. The saddest aspect of that story is that my mum, dad, and sisters never came to watch me play again. I was all for that decision to be honest, as I felt I wouldn't concentrate on my game, knowing that they might be suffering verbal abuse.

My mum and my dad had travelled independently to post-war Britain and integrated into a troubled country with grace and humour. Take them to a football match in 1980s London though, and they feel so awkward, so we agree they shouldn't do it again. It doesn't seem right, does it?

I went home to Karen and Liam that night with a heavy heart and it was an unsettled feeling that never really left me during my time at QPR. I always felt I was on the periphery of not only the starting XI but also the squad. I wasn't treated badly but I did feel I wasn't given any help. Maybe I had been spoilt at Fulham, maybe in the top flight you were simply expected to hit the ground running.

At Craven Cottage I had the likes of Tony Gale, who was always on hand to offer advice, even on the pitch where he would almost coach me though games. That support had gone. Karen felt the same and found it hard to find common ground with the other wives and girlfriends. They would talk about possible nose jobs, and she couldn't quite understand that. The mohican might have gone, but Karen wasn't thinking about a surgeon's knife.

Most of the players lived on one housing estate, a gated community. As players became more senior within the squad, they would move up to the nicer, apparently more grand home. Karen and I still lived in West Norwood. There was also a drinking culture, which was no bigger than at any other club, but I missed Fulham's nights at the Hammersmith Palais where there was a real mixture of players.

As I say, I was the only black player there. I'm not saying that was why there was a distance between me and the lads, but I did feel more comfortable when Les Ferdinand arrived a year after me. I would have to get on with things though. Pull my socks up, and graft if I was to break into the first team as a regular.

The fans saw that I was working. A cheer would go around the tight little stadium each time I rose from the dugout to warm up, and in Jim Smith I had a good manager. Very much from the old school, Jim never discriminated. If you messed up in training or in a game you were a cunt. Simple as that. Whoever you were.

Jim had a bit of a short fuse and with the dugouts back then being so low, he would often jump from his seat too quickly and on several occasions he would come to the touchline to give you a bollocking, but you'd find it hard not to laugh when you saw a slow trickle of blood weaving its way down his bald head.

Jim had a good team but we were hard to gauge. What was obvious was we were far better on the plastic pitch than we were on grass. Prior to Jim's arrival I believe the team went three months when they won one week and lost the next. On merely the plastic, we might have won the league! We would train on it on a Friday afternoon and work mostly on the defence pushing up a high line, knowing full well the ball would speed through on the unnatural surface.

You'd see players, the country's best players – the likes of Bryan Robson and Ian Rush – arriving and walking on to the pitch with a grimace, wondering what footwear to wear and dreading the cuts that would be inflicted on their legs should they attempt a sliding tackle. And you had to tackle. I had the nastiest burns on my knees and arse. The thing was, as teams struggled to play on our plastic, we were awful on the grass, rarely winning away from Loftus Road.

That's why I got so frustrated. At home, I felt Gary Bannister's pace was ideal for the surface but away I wanted to be given more of a chance. Maybe if we changed our style away from home we might win a few more points on our travels. Instead I had to continue to mainly warm the bench and it was frustrating.

The most frustrating match on grass was on the country's most famous grass pitch. In April 1986, we reached the final of the League Cup – or Milk Cup as it was then known – where we played Jim's former club, Oxford United, at Wembley.

We'd beaten title challengers Chelsea in the quarter-final and the eventual champions Liverpool over two legs in the semis and were off to Wembley. For a club of QPR's size, a second major final in the decade was a great achievement but I found it hard to be too enthusiastic when it became obvious I would be sub once again.

On a vast pitch like Wembley, I would have loved to be given the chance of holding the ball up, bringing team-mates into play, but no, Jim went with the norm and it was a tracksuit for me. What I remember most about that day was the surreal coach ride to the stadium. When we reached Wembley Way, Jim stood up at the front of the bus and produced this monkey puppet on the end of his arm for what would be the strangest team-talk in the history of team-talks.

'What's the score going to be today, mate?' he asked his ape. Us players just looked around at each other wondering what was going on. Then the monkey started to talk as Jim put on this weird, croaky voice.

'Three-nil today, boss. It'll be easy!' Cue very awkward laughter and shifting on seats. That monkey was right though. The thing is we lost 3-0.

We were battered by a very good Oxford side including Ray Houghton, John Aldridge, Malcolm Shotton and Kevin Brock. They were so dominant on the day and we never got a look-in. I got off the bench at 2-0 for the last half an hour but we were never in it. It was a disappointing day but being Jim's former club and former players, you could see that he was pleased for them. 'Don't worry, lads,' he said as he came in the dressing room. 'We might have lost but we'll have a much better party than them!' Unlike his monkey's prediction, this time Jim was spot on as we partied late into the night in our London hotel.

The rest of the season fizzled out a bit, notable mostly for a 6-0 win over Chelsea that extinguished our local rivals' faint title hopes. I scored that afternoon but in all it had been an unenjoyable first season. I was still young and at a First Division club so wasn't expecting to be the first name on the team sheet but sitting in a tracksuit most weeks was getting me down.

People often want to know the inner thoughts of a long-term substitute. Do you want the guy keeping you out of the team to get injured? Do you want the team to lose? I can't say I ever wanted these things to happen. In an ideal world, I wanted the team to be playing badly, to come on and score the winning goals.

The mad thing was, there were times when we didn't play well and there were times when I scored but the next week I was back on the bench. That got on my nerves back then but I know now that strikers can't play well every week, they aren't consistent beasts, and that is why breaking into a settled partnership was always going to be hard. As I've said though, it was away from Loftus Road and that pitch that I felt we were weak, powder puff in fact, and that I should have been given a chance to lead the line in a team playing a different way. I think the players wanted a Plan B too, but Jim never took a chance on one, relying I think too much on our home form.

The team was full of big characters like Gary Bannister and John Byrne up front, John Gregory, Steve Wicks and of course Terry Fenwick, and as a young player I felt that sometimes that big presence within the camp overrode a player's ability, making it harder for a younger player or a fringe player to be given a chance. Plenty of players knew they wouldn't be dropped, due to sheer weight of personality rather than good form.

Dispirited, I went back for the next season just hoping something would go my way. It was the summer of 1986 and I remember being fascinated with Terry Fenwick who had played a key role in England's World Cup push in Mexico. More importantly he had been close up to Diego Maradona, a kind of footballing unicorn and we were all eager to know exactly what this footballer was like in the flesh.

Terry was frustrated with how close England had got but he admitted that the little Argentinean was like nothing he'd ever played against. Terry had got into the team thanks largely to an injury suffered by the excellent Mark Wright, but having got in he was impressive and as ever would have organised the team well next to the more dominant Terry Butcher.

For Maradona's second goal, I watched in awe and recall him running at Terry, but with Terry being on a yellow card he couldn't tactically take him out (something he was fond of doing). Although, I'm not sure he would have got close even if he had tried.

The season started badly (on grass!) with a 5-1 defeat at Southampton but the dressing room had become a nicer place as Les Ferdinand and David Seaman had been bought that summer and I hit it off with both of them. David is a great guy, a big, laid-back Yorkshireman who never stopped giggling. And what a goalkeeper too, the best I ever played with. He was just so dominant and it was clear even then that this guy would go on and have a big career.

His driving was less impressive and not long after he joined he treated me to another scary episode that ranks alongside the Malcolm Macdonald 'spin' when I was at Fulham. David had bought a new Audi Quattro and was very proud of it. 'Jump in, Leroy,' he boomed. 'I'll show you what it can do.'

That should have been the warning sign, but I got in and off we went. Next thing I know we're doing 150mph on a dual carriageway. I clearly wasn't built for a life in Formula One because I was clinging to my seat for dear life. David, that big smile emerging from under his moustache, simply giggled and put his foot down.

David would have ample opportunity to show off his goalkeeping skills in his first season as the club suffered, struggling as usual away from home but not finding it as easy on the plastic either. Perhaps opponents were getting used to the plastic and while we won the majority of games, the season was tough and we finished 16th in the table.

I continued to have a peripheral role and began to wonder about my future. I wasn't the type to go and bang on Jim's door and demand to play. I was feisty and would argue my corner but when it came to team selection I knew that shouting wasn't going to help my cause.

Strangely the fate of my two clubs looked intertwined at one point that season when it was reported that QPR and Fulham would merge as one combined outfit. Both were being run by David Bulstrode, who revealed plans to build houses on Craven Cottage and form a new club at Loftus Road. The idea of a Fulham Park Rangers, understandably, didn't go down well with either set of fans and when Jimmy Hill stepped in, heading a consortium at Fulham, the proposals lost all credibility and were rightly shelved.

In the summer of 1987, QPR told me they wanted me to stay and would offer me a new contract. Flattered and determined to get a regular shot at First Division defences, I was ready to sign, knuckle down and give it another go but as I met the manager and the chairman to do just that, they instead informed me that they had changed their minds and I was to be a makeweight in a deal that saw Paul Parker and Dean Coney move the other way. Thank you and goodbye.

It was a blow but because I was heading back to familiar territory, a place where I knew everyone and they knew me, I felt I could get my head down and start again. There was frustration and disappointment though. I so wanted to get a good run in QPR's team but it was never to be and I was now not a top-flight footballer. In fact I would play in the third tier as Fulham had been relegated in 1986 but this was a chance to play, to play every week and that was really all I ever wanted to do. It turned out to be the best thing that could have happened to my career.

The great new thing about Fulham on my return was Jimmy Hill. Jimmy took me for dinner in a restaurant just off Putney Bridge and to be in such a familiar setting, around his enthusiasm for life and the game, was infectious. He loved the club but he so loved football. No bullshit. No empty promises. No grandeur. Let's see what we can do together and let's do it for the love of the game. I've never know a man so enamoured with our sport and he saw things within it and within its people that no one else could.

My old team-mate Ray Lewington was now manager at the club so all in all the familiarity of the place made it the easiest of moves and that showed on the pitch as I settled straight back in, scoring 22 goals in 39 appearances and finishing as top scorer, no mean feat when you're playing up front with Gordon Davies.

Yes, it was a couple of steps down from the First Division, but I went back to Fulham a different player, a more single-minded striker who while happy to be back at Fulham was a more selfish goalscorer. After QPR, I had so much to prove and I knew that goals at Craven Cottage would lead to another go at the top flight.

Jimmy Hill and the club were so good to me, even giving me a wage increase which was unbelievable considering I had moved from the top to the third tier. I was the main man and everyone at Fulham loved me. It felt good. Young players looked up to me and the senior players respected me. It all clicked.

As pleased as I was with my form, I wasn't harbouring thoughts that I had found my level, that this was it, I was a Third Division goalscorer. I still had ambitions and fortunately this was an age when top-flight teams were more than ready to throw their nets into deeper water and take a chance on lower league players, and before that season was out, First Division teams came fishing for me.

7

Sorry Elton, It's Hammer Time

A Bristol hotel, towards the end of my playing career.

I'm standing in the hotel lobby and I notice two guys walk in. Their shaven, bullet-shaped heads catch the sunlight as their eyes catch mine.

One pokes the other with his elbow and they both start to stare. 'Here we go,' I think. 'Trouble.' I start to scan the lobby for security or better still a fire exit when they start to move towards me. 'Right, Leroy. Be cool. Stand your ground. Don't take any shit'.

They approach and flank me, one on each shoulder. 'You're Leroy, aren't you?' one asks, his breath warming my cheeks.

'That's right.'

'Leroy Rosenior?'

'Yes, that's me.' My fists are clenched.

The other guy reaches into the inside pocket of his jacket. This is it. What's he got? He takes out a business card and hands it to me. On it are the words 'THE ICF' and a phone number.

The ICF. West Ham's notorious Inter City Firm. 'Great to meet you, Leroy,' the guys say. 'If you ever need anything, anything at all, just call that number. You're one of us.'

It's not often a Third Division footballer takes a phone call from Elton John. Or at least I don't think it is. Having grown up with Gary Glitter's son, I was well used to small talk with glam rock superstars but still, even I was surprised as I sat on the phone talking to Mr John, sitting attentively as he tried to sell me the virtues of a life at Watford Football Club.

To be fair, it worked. Elton was so enthusiastic about his club and I of course admired what they had achieved throughout the 1980s. I had loved being back at Fulham but everyone, Jimmy Hill, my team-mates, the fans, all of them would understand my wanting another crack at the First Division. A real crack.

Having chatted to Elton and agreed in my mind to go, I spoke to the club officials about the small print to my deal and there came the snag. 'So, when you sign we'll set you up with temporary accommodation before you buy a house near the training ground.'

'Excuse me?' I said.

'You'll have to live within a seven-mile radius of the club when you sign. Club rules.'

A pause. I couldn't believe it. Karen and I were settled in south London. Karen was happy, Liam was happy, as was our new baby, Daron. This wasn't going to work. Watford were shocked that I would pull out of top-flight football because of where I lived but it was a deal-breaker. I wasn't going to Watford. Fortunately another club were ready to move in.

It was March 1988 and the old transfer deadline was fast approaching. One club in desperate need of a striker was West Ham. Having sold Frank McAvennie to Celtic, they had been short of firepower, or more importantly a foil for Tony Cottee. A young Paul Ince had been pushed up front, as had Alan Dickens. Every day the papers reported possible targets like Peter Davenport, Lee

Chapman, Nico Claesen and John Fashanu. So many reported moves had not materialised that the *Daily Mail* nicknamed the club 'The Lepers of Football'.

A £1.5m move for Chelsea's Kerry Dixon was very close but collapsed at the last minute so, having scored those 22 goals – albeit in the Third Division – they turned to me, and better still I could live wherever the hell I wanted. Just turn up to training on time and score goals on a Saturday.

John Lyall, the West Ham manager, rushed to Fulham's training ground on the Thursday to make sure I could play on the Saturday. The deal was done and I was registered and available for selection. The opponents? Watford, of course.

Back in the big time and on £750 a week, not bad at all. A car. A three-year contract. But most importantly I was in a team where I was going to get a fair crack at things. Did I expect to be playing every week? No, of course not, but unlike at QPR I got the feeling from John Lyall that I would get a chance to prove myself. His team needed goals. Badly. Relegation was looming its ugly head. 'Get in there, Leroy,' John said. 'Get in there, create space, create havoc and score me some fucking goals.'

'It was me who suggested Leroy to John [Lyall]. It was a frustrating time. Players were approached but wages seemed a sticking point and you could tell the manager was getting frustrated. John came to me and as a centre-back he asked who I felt would be a good striker to go for. Plenty of First Division strikers had been looked at but I said, why not go to my old club and look at Leroy. He was scoring goals and having watched Leroy a couple of times at Fulham, he liked what he saw. John had an eye for a player and so Leroy joined me at West Ham.'

Tony Gale, West Ham team-mate

I walked into the Boleyn Ground, excited but nervous. I'd never met my new team-mates, let alone trained with them and I knew the away support wouldn't be happy. Watford fans thought I'd turned my back on them for bigger wages at West Ham but as I strolled into my new surroundings, I was more concerned with how the locals would take to me. After all those newspaper reports about top First Division strikers coming, they instead had me, from little old Fulham. The goals had dried up and if I was to misfire early on, well, the guys on the Chicken Run weren't exactly shy when it came to expressing their views.

The omens were good. Liam had been born at home while his grandma and I sat downstairs watching *EastEnders* and then weirdly, as a baby, he couldn't settle to sleep unless we played him the soap opera's theme tune. Footballers will clutch at many straws and this one was firmly in my hands as I walked into the home dressing room.

Immediately I was at ease. You worry sometimes coming into a new dressing room. Players get twitchy that you might be there to replace them but at West Ham, it was obvious they needed another striker. I had arrived, not quite as a saviour, but a striker at last and from the moment I sat down, I felt good.

Liam Brady – a superstar – was getting changed which was a bit scary but the first words I heard came from my old mate from Fulham, Tony Gale. Tony was always vociferous before a game and his loud tone set me at ease. 'You're gonna be great, Leroy,' he said.

'Just come short and get the ball from me, or spin round like we used to do at Fulham. I'll find you. I always did.' To be fair, he was right. He then went off to the toilets to be sick. Again that put me at ease as Tony always did that. The most confident man around but he would always puke prior to kick-off. It's a funny old game.

'Yeah I would do that but it was great to have Leroy there. I told all the lads in the dressing room, get it in to Leroy.

He's a great target man, but for fuck's sake, don't play it to his feet, chip it into his chest! Leroy settled in immediately. The lads could see quickly that he was not only a good player but he was going to work for the team.'

Tony Gale

I looked around and wondered how this team were so perilously close to relegation. They had Liam Brady, Alan Dickens, Tony, Alvin Martin, Tony Cottee, Ray Stewart, Alan Devonshire, and Julian Dicks had signed the day before too. John Lyall was giving the team-talk. Everything seemed right. Time to get out there and make sure it stayed that way.

'It was great to have Leroy there, because what he would give us was a work rate that I felt was missing. In my view too many of the West Ham players were going through the motions and living off the season, two years before, when they came third. All the good things they had done that season had stopped and that included hard work. We didn't do much in training on defending but the team had worked hard. That had stopped. There were overweight players, and a lack of that work. That wasn't necessarily John Lyall's fault, I felt the players needed to do more.'

Stewart Robson, West Ham

The Watford fans gave me the expected stick but the West Ham faithful got behind me from the off, almost praying that every run I ventured and every leap I made would lead to that precious commodity that had deserted their lives; goals.

Half-time and no goals. An hour in, no goals. But then, the ball runs free towards the Watford penalty box and off the shoulder of my defender I'm away. I take the ball in my stride and everything slows down, the noise of the crowd becomes a faint and dull murmur. I look up. Tony Coton in the Watford goal. A big man. Effectively and annoyingly narrowing his angles. Quick Leroy, think.

Blast it. The keeper's done his job so just hit it hard. Crack. I smash the ball and it goes under Coton in goal and into the tight rigging (I always loved how tight the nets were at West Ham due to the proximity of the terracing). Suddenly the noise is back and it's deafening. Pandemonium as my new team-mates swamp me under a collapsed wall of claret and blue.

As I reappear from a pile of love, the fans chant my name. 'Leroy! Leroy! Leroy!' Little did I know it but when the radio transistors reported my goal around Craven Cottage that day, the Fulham fans chanted my name too in appreciation of their guy's efforts. It was a wonderful moment that sealed a 1-0 win but also meant I had hit the ground running. When I wrote in the previous chapter about my time at QPR, I described how I felt uncomfortable and unsettled. This was the very antithesis of that time. From the off, that silky West Ham shirt just felt good on me. Like silk to QPR's static nylon.

> 'I remember those as very happy days. I was young, but I can remember Saturday mornings. Mum would make a big fry-up for dad, and we'd all drive from Streatham, through the tunnel to east London. Dad would sign autographs which I thought was weird, and he would take Daron and me through the treatment room, into a little gym that the players warmed up in. The smell of Deep Heat, the curse words, Liam Brady stretching. I knew then that I wanted to be a footballer.'
>
> **Liam Rosenior**

The great Bobby Moore, now observing from the press box, wrote in his match report that I was 'a class act', which was such a boost and the following week, I scored an equaliser – a good volley – at Old Trafford. Alas, we lost 3-1 to Alex Ferguson's side but I scored again in my third game, this time against Sheffield Wednesday. 'Leroy! Leroy! Leroy!' Things were going great.

> 'As a playmaker in the team it was great to have Leroy. I had arrived a year earlier but it was a tough time at the club because players, good players were wanting to leave. Frank [McAvennie] had gone and Tony Cottee wanted to follow. John Lyall wouldn't have been used to that. He'd grown up at and managed a club where players, wonderful players, were happy to stay. Not anymore. Paul Ince was up and coming and while not looking to leave, he soon would. John went looking for bargains and what Leroy gave us immediately was enthusiasm. It was great to have a target man who would hold it up and we, like the crowd, took to him straight away.'
>
> **Liam Brady, West Ham**

The team needed more wins to stay up but I felt very much part of that fight, and fight I would. Maybe too much. In May, Chelsea came to Upton Park, fearing the drop themselves. This was a fixture that needed no extra needle but with points so desperately at stake, the atmosphere that Saturday in the old ground was particularly exuberant. Our dressing room had been electric before the game and we played brilliantly, getting into the Chelsea team from the off; obeying our fans' demands for nothing less than our all.

I feel great as I battle Chelsea's big centre-backs, linking well with my team-mates, trying to get Tony Cottee in but feeling a threat myself. I score two goals. The fans chant my name. We're winning but I'm hungry. Hungry for a hat-trick. Hungry for the win. Towards the end of the game I go for a strong challenge and while on the ground, Steve Clarke, Chelsea's Scottish full-back, treads on my ankle. 'He's done that on fucking purpose.' The red mist descends.

Next thing I know, my hands are around Clarke's neck. What am I doing? I let go and give the referee the old look of innocence. He gives me a red card. I'm off. Then, as I walk to the tunnel, the biggest cheer of my career goes around the whole ground. 'Leroy! Leroy! Leroy!' I've scored two in a 4-2 win but better still I've strangled a Chelsea man. 'Leroy! Leroy!' Even better still, the win means we'll stay up and Chelsea will eventually go down. *You're one of us.*

Not even that summer's pre-season could dampen my spirits. West Ham just felt right for me and not only because the majority of that summer with John Lyall was with the ball at our feet. I loved it. The thing about working at West Ham was that John and his brilliant staff put you in an environment where you learnt every day. Nothing complicated, just simple stuff but I left every day feeling educated.

They taught you how to pass, when to pass and how to pick the pace of pass. It wasn't drilled into you, in fact they didn't even make a big deal of it, but the sessions were all geared around those fundamental basics.

People scoff at West Ham's sometime nickname, the Academy. Firstly, the club never came up with that label, that was outsiders, but the word is 100 per cent accurate. You felt like you were always being taught. All the time. Even the best first team player. When Sam Allardyce was manager there and under pressure, he questioned the idea of the so-called 'Academy'. I understand that he was under pressure to win football matches, and perhaps in his mind at any cost, but to belittle the very fabric of the football club was, in my mind, disrespectful and rightly upset many people.

The term 'Academy' isn't just about playing pretty football on a Saturday. People called it that because there is an ideology running right through the very core of the place. It started when players arrived as boys. Tony Carr brought so many great players up in the West Ham way and that way continued up to working with the likes of John and his staff, Mick McGiven and Ronnie Boyce, all ex-West Ham players.

Young players were taught the basics that when put into practice each week are attractive to watch but they aren't taught for purely aesthetic reasons. Play the game their way and the feeling is, results will follow.

The fans at the club want to see the game played in a certain way and whatever we did in training, you knew that the very youngest players there were being told similar things. Now, I get that the first team has its own pressures and there are times when you have to adapt and dig in to win a game – that's what Allardyce did – but to suggest the club's ethics are somehow up for debate was wrong.

Clubs today talk about Barcelona and how their youth teams are taught to play the same way as the first team. They talk as if this is somehow progressive and innovative. It isn't. West Ham have been doing it for 50 years. That's why so many players make such a seamless move from the lower ranks into the first team.

One such player was Tony Cottee. Tony was West Ham through and through. He loved the place but that summer he left to join Everton in what was a then British record transfer fee of £2.2m. I was gutted to see him leave. Tony just lived for goals and I had such respect for his single-mindedness. Like Gordon Davies at Fulham, Tony was all about goals, but no disrespect to Gordon, he did it to a much higher degree.

Tony had a little book in which he would write a small description about each of his goals:

'Left foot volley'.

'Back post header'.

'Right foot toe-poke'.

He was obsessed and that suited me down to the ground. Since joining Fulham, raw and eager, and working under Ray Harford, I had become equally obsessed with playing the role of a deeper-lying number nine. With Tony, I could revel in all that I had learnt. I was the first point of call for an attack. The defenders and midfielders could look up and pick me out. I would fight to keep possession, give the ball back the way it came knowing that Tony would have made an intelligent run in behind me, or turn myself and flick the ball on, again knowing that Tony would be doing the right things to test our markers.

Tony though had gone and once again the club needed a goalscorer. David Kelly had been even more prolific than me in the Third Division with Walsall the previous season and maybe buoyed by how nicely I had settled in, the club opted for his services. I loved David. He was the nicest, funniest guy and a very good player. You could see in training just how natural he found goalscoring but after getting off to a slow start, he struggled for momentum and the West Ham fans never saw just how potent he could be.

It's a big step up from the Third Division to the top flight. David was arguably a better goalscorer than me but I came in, I had had some experience at QPR and I got off to a great start. That can be the difference. At the start of the 1988/89 season I continued to feel good, scoring goals and contributing to the team. I had got used to playing against the best centre-backs in the country. I loved the physical side of things and understood that you have to give as good as you get because you get a lot.

There were defenders like Kevin Moran, Steve Foster and Eric Young at Wimbledon. These big guys wore headbands not because of some old injury or for heading the ball. No, they knew that the first challenge in a game meant heading the back of a striker's head. Crack. Have that. I got wind of their game and would love that first jump. Up went the elbow or the forearm, make it look like it's to aid your jump and whack, hit them before they hit you.

> 'What I noticed about Leroy when he came to West Ham was how physical he had become, how nasty even. Leroy is the nicest bloke you'll meet off the pitch. A gentleman. Some might ask was he too nice but fuck that. On the pitch he was hard as nails. He'd learnt to compete, the forearm, have that. The elbow, bosh. I was very impressed and just happy I was on his team and not marking him.'
>
> *Tony Gale*

You had to match the physicality of the game and its hard protagonists and maybe that was lacking with us at West Ham. Our team were such a good side individually but we were missing something, we had a soft underbelly because we weren't very potent when we didn't have the ball. For all the great footballers we had, we needed to get into people's faces more than we did. That's why I understand Sam Allardyce's predicament about trying to win games, but at West Ham it mustn't be at the cost of everything else.

That autumn we twice played Liverpool, under Kenny Dalglish at the time, at Upton Park. They had John Barnes, Peter Beardsley, Ian Rush back from Italy, Steve Nicol, Ronnie Whelan; wonderful footballers who could kill you doing just that, playing football. For a league game they came to us and beat us by the easiest 2-0 scoreline you'll see. They toyed with us like full-up cats playing with a terrified mouse.

A few weeks later they came back for a League Cup tie and we knew what had to be done this time if we were to stand a chance. John had let us know but none of us needed telling. Let them simply play, try to match our football with theirs and we will get beat. We had to play our game when we had the ball but at a very quick tempo and when they had the ball we had to hit them hard early. That's what we did. Paul Ince was on fire and scored a hat-trick in a 4-1 win but the performance proved nothing more than a frustrating insight into what we might have been, rather than a template for what we were.

Too often, playing very well, we lost matches. The football we played was the right football but when we didn't have the ball we looked as pretty as when we had it! It was frustrating, knowing the problem but finding we couldn't put it into practice. John and his staff only knew how to play one way, and try as we might, regular defeats meant another relegation battle was on the cards.

> 'Yes, we struggled without the ball but don't forget that we had an awful injury crisis that season. Big players missed great chunks of the season and for a club like West Ham back then, that was going to hurt.'
>
> **Tony Gale**

Our form in the cups though spoke volumes for the kind of team – great on its day – we were. In January 1989 we drew Arsenal, the champions elect, and a replay at Highbury proved to be one of my most memorable nights in football. George Graham had built an Arsenal team good enough to challenge Liverpool for the top honours. They were a quick, young side who could kill you on the break but unlike us they defended like concrete Trojans.

That night at Highbury though, we matched them. We kept it compact and tight, keeping our potency on the break and not allowing them the space they loved to exploit. With time running out, Liam Brady, upon the surface on which he used to dazzle the locals, looked up and swung in a ball with that wand of a left foot. It was cleared but Dickens hooked it back in and I was on hand to nod it past John Lukic. The 5,000 or so fans who had travelled from the East End went crazy while we kept our heads to clinch a famous win.

> 'That was a great night for me. Going back to Highbury was always going to be special. We had been 2-0 up at Upton Park but I think Paul Merson got a couple and so we went to north London expected to lose. Leroy was a clever forward. If I got the ball in the last third, he was always looking to make his move and we developed a good understanding. I saw from the corner of my eye that he had darted in, I lofted it in to the box with my left foot but the cross was partially cleared. There was a bit of a scramble but being a great poacher, Leroy scored.'
>
> **_Liam Brady_**

Weeks later, I had to visit Brixton police station to answer for a low-level traffic offence. The sergeant sent to question me looked at my name on his paperwork, looked at me and said, 'Leroy Rosenior? Didn't you score the winner at Highbury a week or so ago?'

'That's right,' I said.

'Let's let this one go, mate, and send you on your way.' To this day I'm not sure if that policeman was a joyous West Ham fan or just a relieved Spurs supporter.

Apart from the results in the league, life was so sweet during my time at West Ham and that stemmed mainly from how at home I felt in the kit and in the dressing room. We had a brilliant bunch of lads. Julian Dicks had signed the day before me and was a great, if slightly mad guy. Great player though and so much more than the volatile hard man many have him down as.

You would arrive into training at Chadwell Heath and every day, every single day, you would get changed to the sound of K-Thud. Over and over again. K-Thud. K-Thud. K-Thud. That was Julian in the indoor gym smashing the ball against the wall with his left foot over and over again. Basically, he was working on his strong foot!

We had Mark Ward, a scallywag but a lovable one. Mark was very much part of the club's card school which was a regular part of away trips and he seemed to win far more than he lost. He later admitted in a book that he cheated. You couldn't help but love him though and I was sad when he had troubles after he retired. He was a great player. He used to drive crosses in and I loved attacking them, knowing that all I had to do was get my head on them because he'd generated all the power.

That season, the club spent money buying Frank McAvennie back from Celtic. Macca was some character and turned up to the 1991 FA Cup semi-final in a stretched limo! He'd spend hours after games, blow-drying that mullet of his, curling the ends to perfection but he'd look at me moisturising my skin and grimace. 'Wha' da fuck are ye doin' big man?'

'Moisturising. It's cocoa butter,' I'd answer. Macca would laugh. The thing is today I have lovely, moist skin and Macca has no hair!

Influenced no doubt by Macca and his Page Three girlfriend, Jenny Blyth, we'd all hit the Phoenix Apollo nightclub in Stratford (not far from the club's new ground) or on to Tots in Southend. In either we'd party like rock stars. Well, we'd party with the cast of *Birds of a Feather* and Nigel Benn but it was the funnest of times. I'd come out of my shell, and rid of the awkward feelings I might have had at Fulham and QPR, I could even unleash the odd move on the dance floor.

'I remember Leroy taking me to a West Ham Christmas party. On one hand, he wasn't afraid to tell a bouncer at any club about who he was to jump a queue but he was also very humble. We went to this party and there was Frank

> McAvennie getting out of his limo with two Page Three
> girls, and we jumped off the back of a bus.'
>
> **Martin Loveday**

Martin and George Parris, a great big hulk of a player with a great
touch and an engine to match, were my partners in crime. Like
me, George wasn't a beer drinker but while I was happy with my
Malibu, George had us all wondering just how he managed to
drink a brandy and Bailey's mix.

> 'Today we wouldn't get away with what we got away with
> back then. Too many cameras!'
>
> **Tony Gale**

On the pitch, we continued to struggle as did one individual in
particular, Allen McKnight. Alan had been bought as cover for
Phil Parkes, but injury to our experienced number one meant a
run in the team. That didn't bother us. Allen was an international
goalkeeper with Northern Ireland and you could see from training
that he had talent. He was a good lad, confident around the guys,
but when one high-profile mistake followed another, you could
see a light slowly go out.

The papers smelt blood and soon the headline
'McKNIGHTMARE' was following him to games, where opposing fans were quick to take advantage. It was hard to watch. We
knew his confidence had gone and whether you like it or not, and
however supportive you try to be, the team's can go too, especially
when it's your goalkeeper who is the one suffering.

Results were as bad as Allen's morale. We were still struggling
to make life difficult for teams. Still we played great stuff, still
we could dominate possession but still, the tempo in which
we sometimes attacked was never replicated in how we would
defend.

I had got injured but came back fit and hoping to score the goals that might help us beat the drop. It was a nervous squad and you could see the pressure was getting to the manager. John Lyall was a legend at West Ham. He had played for the club, coached under Ron Greenwood and won the FA Cup in 1975 and 1980. The idea of him being somehow under the cosh and even fearing the chop was incredible.

I never thought his job was on the line because of what he had achieved and just how much a part of the club he had become, but football was changing as the 1990s approached. Chairmen were becoming twitchy and even the Hammers fans were voicing their concerns toward the manager as we edged closer to relegation.

One of those last games was at Sheffield Wednesday. Hillsborough, just weeks after that word had become forever more synonymous with tragedy with 96 Liverpool fans ultimately dying as a result of that disaster but us footballers had to somehow put that to one side and focus on the trivial matters of goals, three points and staving off relegation (and they call the latter a disaster).

It was a very strange afternoon when we went there. You are professional and you know you have a job to do but as we ran out and looked left towards the Leppings Lane terracing, empty but for the bent metal and rubble, you were met with the most eerie of sights, and we played a game that matched the mood.

I scored twice (one at the Leppings Lane end) in a 2-0 win but you couldn't celebrate. I just ran back to the halfway line and got on with things. I recall walking off the pitch and glancing again at this archaic structure in which football fans, decent people, had been told to stand to watch the team they loved.

Crumbling concrete, fences and wires. I was immediately back in Brixton as it reminded me of the local prison that I walked past most days of my young life. A prison is somewhere we send people when we don't want them to escape. A prison is a place for people who scare us. This was a sporting venue. I know hooliganism had been a big problem throughout the decade but the vast majority of trouble had not happened in stadiums. If fans wanted to fight they found spaces away from police. It was so rare to have troublesome events in stadiums and the lengths the authorities went to keep fans *imprisoned* was clearly nowhere near worthy of the fans who stood innocently in these Victorian cages.

Twenty-seven years later I was so impressed and proud of the families and the campaigners for the victims who finally got the truth and justice that the establishment had denied them. People can be underestimated. My father was. The establishment look down on people, thinking they are uneducated and that they will go away because their intellect is inferior. These people deserved credit and respect but they didn't get it and that is disgusting. The whole establishment seemed in on it – from the media to Downing Street – but these people stuck at it, they wouldn't go away.

A group of people, mostly parents who wanted the truth to be known, won. Amazing. It was historic, a massive moment in this country's history. Like apartheid ending in South Africa, and civil rights in America, this was Britain's moment. That may sound like hyperbole but for me, what the Hillsborough families have done is huge and it mustn't be allowed to stop there. They have opened the country's eyes to the wrongdoings of the establishment and for that history must judge them all as heroes.

Football had chosen to go on and at West Ham, with relegation looming we had games to play and win. After taking all the points at Sheffield Wednesday we lost at Everton. I then scored twice in a 2-1 win at Nottingham Forest, one that gave us a chance. It was slim as our last game was at Liverpool who were going for the double but it was a chance nonetheless.

I remember John Lyall sitting us all down and saying that as a club we were an aircraft heading nose first to the ground. 'Right lads,' he said. 'We are all in the cockpit together. The ground is hurtling towards us but every one of us has to [here he started to do the actions of flying a plane] pull this fucker up.'

Unfortunately the damage was done and against a brilliant Liverpool side our plane was doomed. I hit the bar but soon managed to score a good header at the Kop end to bring us level before half-time and to be fair to our spirit, we felt we were in it, hopeful of nicking something against all the odds. Liverpool went through the gears late in the game and after the third goal, we went, losing 5-1 and being relegated.

The dressing room was distraught but the damage had been done long before Anfield. No one can hide the sense of devastation but the overriding emotion when a team goes down is embarrassment. You have to look people in the eye, fans, press, family when you have ultimately failed. You are no longer a top-flight player and that hurts. Especially when you looked at the talent in our dressing room. Today in coaching courses they teach you not to use negative terms like devastated but that's what we all were.

For me there was a double blow. After Liverpool's fifth goal went in that night, I had gone to take the kick-off when I heard a tearing, cracking sound, that sounded terrifyingly like the end. I had been suffering for a while with the knee and when having it drained every Friday before a game I worryingly watched as half a litre of yellow fluid appeared from it. Yes, this was serious. The next day I went to hospital to have the knee drained again but it would be far from that straightforward.

I came to after an operation and my first visitor was the anaesthetist. 'What are you going to do, Leroy?' he asked. I was confused. What did he mean? 'When?' I replied.

'Hasn't the surgeon been in to see you?'

'No.'

The guy looked nervous and I knew something was up. He went on to tell me that I had a hole the size of a 50p piece in my knee and that they strongly advised that I retire. Disaster. I was stunned. I was 25. I wasn't ready to stop but words like cripple were being bandied about and doctors with serious faces can make you think hard about things.

I eventually got back to West Ham and having read the doctor's report they agreed that I should call it a day. John Lyall had sorted me out, rewarding my goals since I arrived with a new four-year deal. The problem was the club hadn't insured me for more than £25,000. That would have been a one-off, lump sum payment instead of my salary, and that wasn't going to cover me in my stupidly premature retirement. The only thing for it was to keep playing and earn my money.

It was all change at the club as John, Mr West Ham, was sacked. It was a shocking decision in my mind but the club felt, having been there so long, maybe he couldn't motivate us any longer. I disagree wholeheartedly and the fact that John went on to be a success at Ipswich – winning them promotion to the First Division just two years later – proved he hadn't suddenly become a bad manager.

> 'That was the most stupid of decisions. John hadn't lost the dressing room and he was still one of the best football men around. In my mind the club paid for that decision for decades afterwards. What we didn't know was that Lou had all these betting allegations behind the scenes. We went from having the best manager we'd ever worked with to having the worst.'
>
> *Tony Gale*

Lou Macari came in. I had been a big fan of Lou as a player and loved the swashbuckling Manchester United team that he graced in the 1970s. Hopes that he would manage West Ham in the same free-flowing manner though were immediately quashed.

Lou brought in some very good footballers, such as Trevor Morley and Ian Bishop, but despite these guys being ball players, he restricted what they could do with it. The training was all about running. I was injured and watched the pre-season amazed at his one-paced running sessions that went on for ages. For the players, many of whom had been at the club a long time, this was not on. There was no zip, no sharp ball work and ultimately no fun. You can't ask the likes of Frank McAvennie to jog and jog and jog and jog and never smile and then produce quality on matchday.

It was a surprise to us all, a generation of players who had grown up watching Lou play. Where was the cavalier approach, where was the fun? Results were as serious as the new regime. We went to Torquay in the FA Cup in January and having had dinner on the Friday night, Lou came over to myself and George Parris and asked us both to get into our shorts and meet him outside.

Both of us were carrying injuries. My knee was still a problem and George had a knock on his ankle. Lou walked us down to the beach and told us to get in. We couldn't believe it. It was dark, it was freezing but in we went, me up to my knees, George just up to his ankle. There we stood for a while in the ice-cold water, looking with puzzled expressions at each other until we were instructed to get out. The next day I was sub and Torquay beat us 1-0. Oh, and George and I got the flu.

Lou clearly wanted to make his mark early. Maybe that was understandable as he was following such a West Ham legend into the manager's office but it was always going to be hard, what with so many senior players around, used to doing things a very different way, and things didn't improve.

Lou was sacked in his first season, just days after a heavy 6-0 defeat at Oldham (on more damn plastic) in the semi-finals of the League Cup. I was injured that night and played in the return game, a 3-0 win but by then the club were looking for a new manager. They didn't look far.

A white wedding! Willie and Gladys tie the knot (for the second time) at Holy Trinity Church in Tooting.

Learning my trade. Turning out in any weather for my school team, Strand Grammar, (left photo, I'm top row second from right) and Stockwell United (I'm middle bottom row)

Check out my collars! Enjoying another party with my mum and dad at Thornbury Road, Brixton.

Butter wouldn't melt. Fulham's new young striker shortly after I signed in 1982.

The first of many. I take the applause from the crowd and the electronic scoreboard having scored on my home debut against Derby County in December 1983.

Daddy Cool! Relaxing with baby Liam.

Referee! I soon realised that professional football was tough.

Suited and booted. My dad and I at a family occasion.

The lone ranger. My time at Loftus Road wasn't the best but there was the odd reward for my efforts.

Not quite a supersub. I only got half an hour at Wembley and was unable to stop Malcolm Shotton and his Oxford United team-mates from winning the Milk Cup.

THAT'S ROSY!

West Ham 1 Watford 0

THINGS look a bit Rosier for West Ham this morning — but only a bit.

New signing Leroy Rosenior scored the winner on his debut and it had everyone at Upton Park singing and dancing again.

But the joy, not to mention relief, shouldn't mask the fact that John Lyall still has a lot of work to do to put things to rights.

They have had so little to celebrate during this depressing season and they were ready for a party for any reason yesterday.

Rosenior, the £275,000 signing who stepped in where six top First Division strikers refused to tread, provided the excuse they needed.

So they chanted his name. And they gave him a standing ovation at the end.

He deserved it, too. He'd had four quick attempts to score before he finally got the goal.

Leroy's ace

By JOHN DILLON

But the reaction from the terraces shows just how desperate West Ham have become for success of any kind.

West Ham's victory — their first in 11 League games — was a desperately close one and those singing, shouting fans would do well to remember that.

Inspiration

Watford had more serious chances and it was only thanks to McAlister that the Hammers kept them out.

Porter caught him off-balance with a 25-yard snap shot but he recovered to punch it behind.

And McAlister moved quickly to stop Blissett's attempt to bundle an equaliser across the line from substitute Roberts's cross.

West Ham, whose form has been atrocious in recent weeks, managed some of the inspiration so conspicuously missing for most of this season.

Ward and Keen were perky enough in midfield and their long passes created chances for Cottee, Robson and Rosenior in the opening half-hour.

A typical long ball that led to the goal. Gale pumped it forward and Rosenior out-stripped two defenders before shooting past Coton.

West Ham might have had another as they finally got on top in the last ten minutes.

Coton did well to stop a diving header from Strodder, and Cottee was close when he turned Terry and shot just wide.

Rosenior said afterwards: "I can play better but I was pleased with my performance.

"It is bound to do me good playing with such quality players, although I felt knackered at the end.

West Ham manager John Lyall said: "It was a very important win for us. It could not have been better than for the new lad to get the winner.

"He could become a favourite. The game is not always about signing the big names — it's about giving the youngsters a chance too."

WEST HAM: McAlister 7 — Potts 7, Strodder 6, Gale 6, Stewart 6 — Ward 7, Robson (wdrn) 7, Bonds 6, Keen 7 — * ROSENIOR 8, Cottee 7. Sub: Dickens 7.

WATFORD: Coton 7 — Gibbs 7, McClelland 7, Terry 6, Rostron 7 — Sterling 7, Sherwood 7, Hodges 6, PORTER 8 — Allen (wdrn) 7, Blissett 7. Sub: Roberts 7.

Ref: R. Lewis 7.

Making the headlines after my dream debut for West Ham in 1988.

You can't blame me for loving my new jacket. It cost most of my new weekly wage at West Ham.

Grandad Bill! Liam enjoys the comfort of dad's arms.

A proud dad! Chilling out with my second son, Daron.

Those days practising with a balloon in the living room paid off! Here I am winning an aerial duel for West Ham against Tottenham in 1989.

*Blowing Bubbles!
I loved my time at
West Ham.*

Shameless advertising. Having got a move to Bristol City I'm joined by my team-mates Martin Scott (bottom) and Keith Welch in plugging a certain fizzy drink.

A good ol knees up! My troublesome knee receives some much-needed acupuncture.

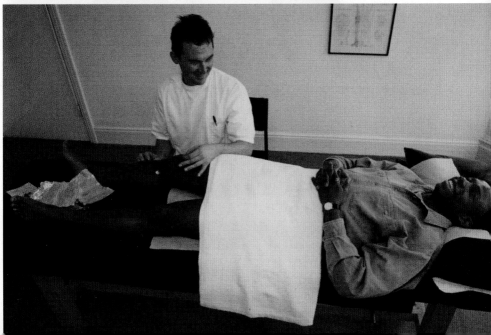

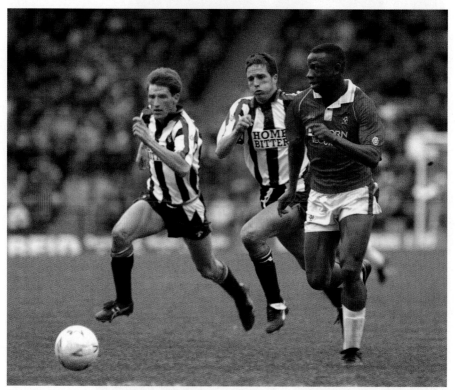

Despite the knee issues I still manage to put the burners on at Notts County in 1993.

Going back to my roots! When the head of the Sierra Leone FA asked me to play for my parents' country, I jumped at the chance.

Coach Leroy! Teaching the stars of tomorrow at Bristol City.

Player boss! A rare outing with Gloucester City where I was the new manager.

Graduation Day as I receive my Pro Licence badge. Notice Tony Adams on the far right.

Mum and Dad proudly hold my sons, Liam and Daron, my nice Rebecca (in my mum's arms) and my nephew, Job (with my father).

Family is everything. Enjoying a reunion with the Roseniors. From left to right, Lorna, Lauren, mum, dad, Lena and Lynda.

Managing with a smile. I immediately settled into life as manager at Torquay.

Taking the applause from the brilliant Torquay fans after a 2-0 defeat in the FA Cup third round at Premier League Birmingham.

To think I was sacked from Brentford for being too nice. My assistant, Paul Mortimer, keeps me out of trouble during a Carling Cup clash with Luton in 2006.

The bees-knees! My time at Brentford was a frustrating one but I learnt a lot about myself and the game.

Say cheese! Content and happy covering football for Premier League Productions.

My mum and dad. I love you both very much.

My team! Ethan, my lovely partner Luci, Max and Millie.

Billy Bonds, like Lyall dripping in claret and blue, came in having done a job for a while with the youth team. Bonzo was great and stepped into the role seamlessly. There was still a bit of running, if only to show off just how fit our new manager was. Billy was a machine, always at the front with the young guys but he also got us playing with a football. Simple but effective and the players responded.

The club had understandably brought new players in up front such as Jimmy Quinn and Mike Small but I was keen to play. Even with my knocks I felt I was better than those two. That's how footballers think but the body was telling me things that I simply wasn't prepared to listen to.

In Bonzo's first full season, not only did we achieve promotion, we got to the FA Cup semi-final where we faced Nottingham Forest at Villa Park. I was unable to play because of the knee but instead joined the thousands of fans in the stands. It was great supporting the team and getting a taste of the fans'-eye view and I was just as annoyed and foul-mouthed at the officials as our supporters who took out their ire on the referee who wrongly sent Tony Gale off early in the game and effectively ruined the contest.

With ten men and their team getting beat, the West Hams fans started to sing 'Billy Bonds's claret and blue army' and despite four goals going against them, they didn't stop and nor did I. There I was, a registered player but singing along with the fans, and it was there I realised just how great, just how unique Hammers fans are, always going that bit further to support the team, even in the midst of defeat.

'Fucking Keith Hackett it was who sent me off. That week had seen a new rule come in about the professional foul. Hackett wanted to be the first one to implement it. Simple as that. Live TV, big match, big audience, look at me, the

big ref with the new rule. I was furious. I'm sorry Hackett
ruined Leroy's day in the stands!'

Tony Gale

I so loved the club and the fans. I think the idea that I had to leave
– however right it was – was one I didn't want to accept. I had
defied the doctors who said I should pack it in and now I wanted
to defy the doubters who presumed my time in east London was
up. Billy was always straight with me though. No bullshit from
Billy, he wasn't cut from that cloth and I always respected him
for his honesty.

West Ham were back in the First Division and my knee,
however much I tried to ignore it, was not getting any better. I
wasn't quitting football though. No way.

* * * * *

Tuesday 10 May 2016 and I'm back, back at the Boleyn Ground
for a night match against Manchester United. Former players
have been invited for what is the final game at the old place and
while I'm privileged to be there, I so wish I was lacing my boots
and getting ready to play. West Ham at home for a night game.
The best place I ever played. The closeness of the supporters, the
noise of 'I'm Forever Blowing Bubbles', the humour, the passion.
For me, it was the ultimate. I loved it and if I could have one
more game anywhere in the world it would be a night match at
West Ham.

There were so many great players there that night and we all
circulate, discussing old times, and great occasions. Eddie is a
fixture at West Ham. He has been there for 50 years. You'd have
seen him on *Match of the Day*, in the background but as much a
part of the place as any of the great footballers. Eddie comes over
to me, puts his arm around me and starts to speak to the guys
around us.

'I've seen some greats here, some of the best, but this kid,' he's pointing at me. 'This kid had it. This kid is the best header of the ball I ever saw.'

I walked out of the ground and thought about what I had achieved and what Eddie had said. I wasn't a Geoff Hurst or a Tony Cottee but I gave everything for the club and the punters who come every week. I wasn't the best of the best, but a guy like Eddie had seen that I had a bit about me. I was good. That was enough for me. That night, as I walked towards my car away from the famous Boleyn Ground for the last time, I thought of those skinheads I had met in Bristol. They were right. I was one of them.

8

Realm Of The Free

Tap…tap…tap.

My father had been expecting an ominous knocking but nevertheless, it filled the house with fear. Minutes earlier he and my mother had peered from behind an upstairs curtain and seen that unwanted visitors were headed their way. They were banging on neighbours' doors and soon it would be his turn.

Tap…tap…tap.

As a kid, when the doorbell went and having peeped from the living room window in Brixton and seen that it was the electricity man come to enquire about a meter skilfully but illegally tampered with, Dad would tell us all to hide and be quiet. Off we'd tip-toe behind the sofa or into the kitchen, trying hard not to squeal with laughter. It was an adventure where our imaginations could run wild until Dad would give the all-clear, 'He's gone. You can come out now.'

This was different. In the late 1990s my mother and father had moved back to Freetown in Sierra Leone to give life a go in the home town that together, they had never called home. The region had been in political turmoil for years and in May 1997 there was a new coup in which Freetown itself was taken easily by a military general, Johnny Paul Koroma, who had been freed from jail by his soldiers and who would oversee widespread looting, rape and murder in the city for months to come.

Moving from door to door, arresting people on a whim and taking them handcuffed into custody, armed soldiers on a mission to fill prison cells and maybe worse were on their fearful manoeuvres. Who knows what fate befell those taken from their homes on that sinister, moonless night and my father knew he and my mum were in trouble. 'Hide,' he told her. 'Hide well.'

He directed her to a small cupboard, gave her a reassuring hug and made an unconvincing promise that he would – like he had so often in London – talk his way out of a tricky situation.

Tap…tap…tap.

My father tentatively answered the door.

* * * * *

'Don't do it!' my dad had always said. Ever since I had started at Fulham, the Sierra Leone national team had made formal and informal contact regarding me playing for their national team. Dad was adamant I shouldn't, citing his country's widespread corruption and unorganised bureaucracy as a reason to simply not get involved. I would nod and smile at him but the real reason I was saying no was I had ambitions of playing for England. As a schoolboy footballer, I had worn that blazer with the three lions and I wanted to do it at a senior level.

Under Graham Taylor I had made one under-21 appearance and while I didn't agree with Graham's style of football, I liked him and wanted to sample international football at a higher level. It wasn't to be. In 1993, in the autumn of my playing career and with an African Nations qualifier against Guinea looming, word reached me that the country of my mum and dad's birth once again requested my services. 'Don't do it!' said my dad with his usual defiance. This time though, I had other ideas.

By now, in 1993, I'd moved to Bristol City and my manager there, Russell Osman came to me saying Sierra Leone had been in touch and that he gave me permission to travel and play, as long as I was back on the Friday for the game the following day. So having consulted my dad and ignored his wishes, I packed my bags for Africa.

As I walked through customs in Lungi airport in Freetown, my first reaction was that Take That must have been there for a concert. Thousands of people were there, a red carpet was laid out and the president was there, plus the press, flash photography, and a stretched limo. 'It's for you,' my escort informed me. As the first guy playing his football in the English game (football's motherland) my appearance had clearly struck a chord. Why didn't I do this earlier, Dad?

Having greeted my people I made my way to a top hotel. It was late at night and in my suite with my kit laid out on the bed – pristine white with a prominent black number nine – I thought only of rest as way of preparation for the following day's game. No chance.

For what seemed ages, scores of people came to my door, each one carrying a dish of food. It was 10pm and I was effectively being given a banquet. Soon my hotel room looked like an all-you-can-eat buffet. 'Hello Mr Rosenior,' they all said. 'Please accept this dish. It will make you strong for the game.'

In Freetown, bringing someone food is the ultimate show of appreciation and while the dishes looked great (mainly cre-cre soup, a sort of spinach-like vegetable popular in these parts) I had no interest in eating it, and not just because they were not a patch on my mum's dishes. I instead called the hotel staff and the food was happily shared around so among. It was nearly midnight but finally I could sleep.

The following morning, slightly jaded but excited to play, I made my way downstairs where hundreds of my fans had come to the hotel. Okay, I'm getting a bit carried away here but this was fun. Crazy, but fun! I boarded the team bus, met my manager and team-mates, none of whom I had ever heard of, and off we went to the hoverport where we would take the hovercraft to Guinea.

If the thousands of excited fans and the treatment I had received since landing hadn't been evidence enough I soon got another taste of how huge football had become in Africa. Just three years earlier at Italia 90, Cameroon had shaken the world, and the game was taking hold of the continent. As we travelled on the hovercraft, I noticed that we passed plenty of purposeful-looking rowers on kayaks, waving to us as we went.

'What are they doing?' I asked my companion.

'Rowing to Guinea for the match.'

'How long does this hovercraft take to get there?'

'Two hours?'

'How long will it take them?'

'Twelve hours.'

I sat and watched these most dedicated of fans and thought of my own dad, who had once rowed out of Freetown bound for Senegal. He might not be that impressed with my decision to play for his country but he would have been proud of both the stamina and dedication of his people.

Once in Guinea, the fervour didn't die down. Fans lined the street, gesturing at us, shouting. These are neighbouring countries and this has the feel of a local derby. The 30,000 all-seater stadium is packed hours before the game (those rowers must have had a hearty breakfast) and having got changed on the bus, we ran out on to the pitch where the atmosphere is incredible.

I've played at Millwall's old Den and led the line for West Ham against Chelsea where relegation is on the line. I've upset Leeds fans and I've silenced Liverpool's Kop but the buzz in this ground was electric. Then our coach gave a short team-talk before handing over to his witch doctor (traditional healer). And I thought the treatment room at West Ham was weird.

One by one, the players were blessed by this guy with all sorts of medicines and paraphernalia. 'Rosenior, you will score goals,' he tells me. I nodded appreciatively but I was more concerned with the heat. It was a boiling evening in Guinea and while my genes were from that part of the world, my climate was Brixton and Bristol. I took on some water and the game kicked off.

Despite being blessed and instructed to score goals by a higher power, I only managed to hit the crossbar in a game that finished 0-0. My main memory of the occasion is playing in front of an all black crowd. For years I'd plied my trade in front of mainly white faces and I'll admit that it was strange to be surrounded by Africans. No bananas were going to be thrown at me here!

After the game I was interviewed by a television channel, then bundled into a car with my kit still on and driven back to the airport. I missed my flight due to supposedly having the wrong visa and after paying out an extra £200 (Dad was right about the corruption) I boarded another plane and I was soon back in England after the most whirlwind of weeks.

My luggage was less fortunate. It would be three months before I saw that (Dad was right about the organisation) but I look back at my international career with a smile and I'm so pleased I did it. They don't give out caps in Sierra Leone and it may have been only three days rather than three lions but I can say that I have been an international footballer.

* * * * *

Tap...tap...tap.

My father tentatively opens the door. Standing there are armed soldiers. 'You are under arrest,' they tell him. 'Who else is here?'

'No one,' my father says.

Rifles are cocked as soldiers look beyond my father and contemplate searching the house. My father stays calm but he knows this is not good. 'You are coming with us.'

They start to lead my father to their vehicle. 'What is your name?'

'Rosenior.'

The soldiers stop. They stop, think and their eyes widen.

'Rosenior? Rosenior? Are you related to Leroy? The Sierra Leone striker?'

'Yes, he's my son.'

'Your son?'

The soldier releases my father's arm and quietly talks to his superior officer before returning.

'Please go back into your home. Wish Leroy well and goodnight.' With that, they're gone.

* * * * *

See, Dad, it wasn't such a bad idea after all.

9

I Loves It, I Do

TUESDAY 23 May 1989. Anfield. The night things cracked. West Ham's eight-year stay in the First Division. Cracked. My knee after years of niggly trouble. Cracked. My feelings about loyalty in football and the notion we're in it together. Cracked. When the medics told me – just months into a new four-and-a-half-year contract – I should pack it in and I discovered that my employers had chosen to insure me for only £25,000, lessons were learnt about how a professional footballer should approach his career.

For my own part, it was late in the day but when my son Liam became a pro, I was on hand to pass on pearls of wisdom about life in the game and the strange relationship between player and club. Don't forget, in 1987, I had walked into a room at QPR expecting to sign a new contract as promised. Instead I left that room having been told I was leaving immediately. That is fine, football works that way.

No, it was hearing that my health and insurance had been valued at such a minimum that underlined the fact and allowed me to tell Liam that in this game, he has to look after number one. Play with nothing but commitment for the team you call

138

home and for the fans who pay to come and see you, but don't expect to be thanked or rewarded for putting your body on the line. I, like so many players, had sacrificed comfort and joints for the cause but the club had valued my career at effectively less than £7,000 a year. *'Sorry, your career is over, Leroy. Thanks for everything. Here's £25,000.'*

My knee was drained every Friday during that relegation run-in at West Ham, eventually taking its toll in the most serious of ways. I never asked for recognition for that; I was desperate to play but the events after the injury in Liverpool proved just what a tough business football can be. It also proved just how tough a human can be.

I love West Ham. I've made that clear. I would have drained more than my knee to pull on their claret and blue every weekend but when people – people who have nothing to do with the actual football side of things – tell you they have valued your career at £25,000 over four years, you wonder about whether that love is requited.

Seven grand a year wasn't going to pay my bills so – with a hole the size of a 50p piece in my knee – on I went. For six months I worked with the club's physio. No disrespect but he was useless. Back then, physiotherapy at even the top clubs was so archaic. The magic sponge culture still prevailed but that sponge had been joined by ultrasound. Physios loved ultrasound. A bit of gel, turn on the machine and off we go.

And the doctors were as keen to use a scalpel as the physio was to plug in the ultrasound. For half a year I had ultrasound and worked on my quads and hamstrings, trying to build up the muscle around the knee. There was little progress but I was adamant that I could play again.

It was my team-mate Stewart Robson who did more for me with one conversation than any medical man had done in months. Stewart knew all about injuries. He had been blighted by them ever since he came on the scene at Arsenal. Once touted as a future England captain and compared to his namesake Bryan, Stewart had been beset by setback after setback, especially in his pelvis. I once watched an operation Stewart had as they videoed it and they took streams of this cotton wool-looking stuff from out of his body. It was scar tissue. After games Stewart would be on crutches and in pain but like me he just wanted to play.

Stewart suggested I go with him to BIMAL, a sports rehabilitation unit in south-west London. I did and it changed my life. It was a revolutionary place. Top sportsmen were regulars there; the likes of rugby league's Ellery Hanley and rugby union's Will Carling. Even Princess Diana was a visitor (other than a strained marriage, her injury isn't clear) so while I would have to pay for it myself, it was money well spent.

They had me on this Cybex machine, on which you do weights but by using speed. They asked if I had been working on my abductors. I didn't even know what abductors were. They basically taught me to run again, a very different style, from my hips rather than my knee. I looked a bit like a slow Michael Johnson but the stress on my knee joint disappeared. I would finish my career shuffling around football pitches but better that than it finishing on a hospital bed.

Stewart and I had had our eyes opened and I think that concerned our bosses. One Friday at West Ham I was with the club doctor, Brain Roper. He examined my knee. 'There's too much fluid on it, Leroy,' he said. 'You're going to have to sit out the match this week.' I was frustrated but shrugged my shoulders and thought I'd have to adhere to the doctor's wishes.

Two minutes later, Roper came back in. 'Actually Leroy, let me have another look. I think I might have been hasty, let's see what we can do to get you out there.' Suddenly, Stewart stormed in with a face like thunder. 'You're a disgrace,' he was shouting. Lou Macari followed him in and while I was wondering what all the commotion was about, Stewart wasn't about to be quiet, quickly turning his ire on to Lou as well. 'You both are. It's a fucking disgrace.'

'What, Stewart?' I asked.

'These two, Leroy. Fucking disgrace. I just heard them. The doctor tells the gaffer you can't play but Lou says he has no other strikers and could he go back in and pass you fit. That ain't on!'

'Treatment rooms at football clubs were a disgrace back then. I had got injured at Arsenal and Gary Lewin, the physio there, didn't have a clue what was wrong with me. They were in the dark at West Ham too and so I took matters into my own hands. Because I researched and found the BIMAL centre and a guy called Alan Watson there, because I worked hard, seven hours a day to get back to fitness, because I was paying for it myself, working bloody hard every day, I was considered a troublemaker. I was shunned by people at the club who didn't trust what I was doing, and I think Leroy was a bit too. Then you have these guys who sit on a static bike machine in the club's little gym, eating a sausage sandwich and watching the telly, smiling at the physio. They were considered good lads. I knew though that like Leroy – if I didn't get the right treatment – I wasn't going to play again. I was proved right because I went to Coventry and won their player of the season a year later. Leroy managed to get a move to Bristol City. That wouldn't have happened if he had sat in the treatment room at West Ham and been a good lad and smiled. You have to look after yourself. Or in those days you did. Especially when it came to injuries and rehab. The treatment he was receiving on his knee was nothing short of a disgrace.'

Stewart Robson

Maybe I should be flattered that Lou wanted me to play so desperately but the concern was that this went on a lot. Players were playing when they weren't anywhere near fit. We all play with niggles and we all want to play but for too long, risks were being taken with players and as Stewart and I clocked on to that – and I think Stewart is right – we were labelled troublemakers.

> 'Leroy bravely carried on at West Ham, and could still do a job but you could see a slight limp developing when he walked. He maintained that brilliant leap of his and scored some goals but the signs were on the wall. With West Ham promoted back to the top flight, I think he knew he would struggle to get into the team.'
>
> *Tony Gale*

We played a game at Villa Park and I just knew that at that level, it wasn't right. Billy Bonds was the new boss and he was nothing but upfront with me. First of all I had gone out on loan purely to get some game time under my belt. That was hard. It felt like a mini knock, a step back. I wasn't young and so going on loan was hard but needs must.

I went to Charlton first. Alan Curbishley later told me I was all he could afford. Curbs was after a bit of experience (on the cheap!) so I got on with things. I also got my first taste of coaching when one morning, a frustrated Alan, having gone over and over a drill, walked off saying, 'Leroy, can you just teach them how to pass the fucking ball?' I did and I loved it.

I also went back to Fulham for the third time and that was probably one time too many. It's always nice to be at Fulham and there were plenty of friendly faces but I didn't score many goals and it felt forced. I was after something more long-term, something more stable so when Bristol City got in touch wanting me to sign permanently, I jumped at the chance.

Denis Smith was the boss at City. He had recently been sacked by Sunderland before taking the job at Ashton Gate. I immediately liked him. He had a nice, northern way about him and was simple about what he wanted from me. 'Get hold of t'ball. Can you do that, Leroy?' Denis said in his Staffordshire tones. I could get hold of the ball, yes. That was that. Three years after being told I had to pack football in, I was signing a two-year contract with a new club.

Denis said not to bother taking the medical – 'You'll only fail it' – so with the minimum of fuss I was off to play football outside the capital for the first time in my career. Joining me from London was a young striker let go on loan by Arsenal and cleverly snapped up by Denis at City to hopefully score the goals that would save the club from relegation.

Andrew (or Andy as he was then known) Cole was recognised in football circles as being a prolific and talented young player. His attitude had been questioned at Highbury though and with the likes of Ian Wright and Kevin Campbell fixtures in George Graham's forward line, he joined me in the West Country to kick-start his career.

Coley and I stayed at the Avon George Hotel near Clifton in Bristol, a smart part of town near the famous suspension bridge. I liked Bristol immediately. It was nice to be out of London, even if the locals might take longer getting used to me. Coley and I would stroll into Clifton and one day I noticed a nice jewellers. I crossed the road and approached the shop window. Suddenly and drastically, the shop's shutters came flying down and the lady working inside – with a panicked look in her eyes – mouthed from behind the shop door that I couldn't come in. I was flabbergasted. I told Coley and he couldn't stop laughing. I wasn't wearing a black and white shirt and holding a bag with SWAG written on it, so I can only guess it was because I'm black. *Toto, I've a feeling we're not in Brixton anymore!*

On the pitch I settled in very quickly. Like West Ham, goals were needed and soon. I chipped in with a few but Coley hit the ground running hard and you could immediately see that he was a top striker. I could simply play deep, 'get hold of t'ball' and let Andy do all the running. Like starting out at Fulham and then at West Ham, I was very much the foil for a more diminutive goalscorer. The fact that doctors had told me to stop just made every second I was playing that much more enjoyable.

In the team – and also helping make life enjoyable – was Dariusz Dziekanowski from Celtic. A Polish international, Jackie – as he was known – was a phenomenal footballer. He was overweight but what a talent. He would do all sorts of tricks. Plenty of players do that flick, where they roll the ball up on to their heel and flick it over their head. I believe it is called a *bicicletta* in South America and Ossie Ardiles made it famous in the film *Escape to Victory*. People will do that in training. Jackie did it in a game and hit the crossbar with a volley. The crowd loved him.

Jackie liked to go out and drink. Not a few beers either. It was vodka and that meant that days would pass with no sign of him. Russell Osman was later manager and it must have been so frustrating but that was the sort of character he had on his hands. Jackie's best days were way past him but Russell will have known that he still had a great talent in his squad. It would just be a case of trying to rein him in, as best he could.

Coley scored eight goals in 12 appearances to keep the club up and I loved playing alongside him. I felt a renewed passion for the game. I loved helping out in defence at set pieces and then getting forward, playing mainly with my back to goal, tussling with centre-halves and creating space for Coley. We went eight games unbeaten and staved off relegation.

My home life was less successful. Karen and I had been drifting apart for a long time but she came to Bristol for what we hoped might be a fresh start. It wasn't to be. Karen might have moved back to London with the boys but she stayed in Bristol and I appreciated that as I obviously wanted to be near them. We got Karen a house very close to mine and like most parents, got on with trying to raise them as best we could.

We had been arguing like cat and dog and eventually it was obvious that divorce was the best option for all of us. Karen was my first love, my first girlfriend. Maybe we got married too soon. We were both teenagers and that can put a strain on things, as can the life of a footballer. I'm not going to blame my profession for the marriage breaking up, but looking back, I understand that I was a distracted husband.

My knee. I guess you could say that that troublesome joint had become like a mistress to me. I obsessed about it. I'd go to bed hoping it wouldn't hurt the next morning. I'd spend the day massaging it, willing it to respond to treatment. I'd measure the swelling, I'd simply look at it, trying to force the swelling down, praying that I'd be able to play that weekend. I wanted to contribute to the team but I also wanted to prove people wrong. Football wasn't to blame for Karen and I splitting up but I do acknowledge that I became distant, self-absorbed, even selfish at that time, and even the move to the West Country wasn't going to salvage the marriage.

We had though salvaged Bristol City's status in what – thanks to the formation of the new Premier League – was now the First Division. The following season was tricky. Coley didn't stop scoring goals, that was the same, but the team was finding it hard. Denis tried to sell Coley, not because he stupidly wanted to strip the club of assets but I felt he realised he had this thoroughbred footballer who was going to leave eventually and, given the right sale and the right amount of money, could help finance the rebuilding of a team in need of several new players.

The club's directors were less keen at first and they clashed with Denis, and we got to think that the relationship between board and manager was a tenuous one. One day though, Coley came to me with a worried expression on his face. 'Leroy, I have a problem,' he said.

'What's up?'

'Newcastle want to sign me. Kevin Keegan has bid nearly £2m and I think City are going to accept.'

'What the fuck are you looking so worried about then, Coley? That's great news.'

I was right. Newcastle under Keegan were on the up. They were in the First Division with us but looked capable of walking it and making waves in the new Premier League. 'The thing is, Leroy,' Coley said, 'I don't have an agent. How am I going to get a good deal?'

It was sweet and a sign of more innocent times but I immediately got on the phone. I never had an agent in my life but I knew people and set Coley up with a guy called Steve Wagott, a Geordie guy who, with the former Celtic and Chelsea defender Paul Elliott, helped Coley with his move, and it's safe to say that our young striker never looked back.

What a player Coley was. You could see that soon, when training with better players, this was a striker who would go to the top. He was a fiery character. That would have raised a few eyebrows in the game but he was young and eager (that eagerness would have been wrongly mistaken for anger and arrogance) to play. Yes, Ian Wright and Kevin Campbell were ahead of him at Arsenal but to Coley, scoring loads of goals in the youth team and reserves, he was better than them both. Even a legend like Wright.

A kid thinking he is better than a club's eventual record goalscorer is chippy, he's arrogant to a fault. A loose cannon. He'll have to move along, the troublemaker. The funny thing is, over time, you could argue that Coley was better than both those players. It's hard to call with Wright, yes, but it's an argument nonetheless.

Coley would strut about. Later he asked to be called Andrew, not Andy. That was arrogant wasn't it? No, it was his name. He never asked to be called Andy so why not inform people that his name was Andrew? He came to Bristol, a big signing from a big club and some might have been suspicious. He had this walk, this way.

He would buy the best clothes, a nice watch, all that. He wore Hugo Boss suits or a jacket and keep the Boss label on the sleeve. 'Let people see what you're wearing.' That always made me laugh. Some might say that's flash, but Coley was just supremely confident. Actually he was very quiet and reserved. In no way was he flash.

What he could do with ease was score goals. We started to train together and he would, from nowhere, shoot from the byline, an impossible angle. I'd tut and start a bollocking. The experienced centre-forward telling the new young buck to get his head up and pass the bloody thing. Before I could start my rant the ball was in the net.

Rants aside, he was very open to advice. We talked about the art of getting into the best positions to score. Andy's finishing was incredible, it was natural. No coaching was needed. But he listened eagerly when it came to positioning. I just told him to save his energy for scoring. I would come deep, get the ball, give it, and Coley was on hand to finish moves off. He was a special player who deservedly won both plaudits and honours.

In the City dressing room I sensed that Coley wasn't the most popular. Maybe I was lucky because we lived in the hotel together for months so I got to know the real Andrew Cole. Big personalities in the squad though – the likes of Mark Aizlewood, Gary Shelton, Andy Dean – didn't like it. They didn't like that Coley wasn't interested in the same things they were.

There was a big gambling culture at the club and Coley just wasn't interested. That made him aloof in their eyes. Here was this young player on the up and perhaps the senior players resented how different he was to them. The fact is though, they wouldn't have seen a better player at Bristol City than Andrew Cole. Did the colour of his skin affect how they treated him? I wouldn't know about that but I'd argue that his being black would have added to the overall perception of him as flash and too full of himself.

Football had changed since the 1980s. John Barnes's move to Liverpool in 1987 had created a sea change. You're not aware of it at the time but looking back, his move to a club who were one of Europe's biggest and most renowned was massive. Sure, there were barriers to knock down once he got there, but attitudes shifted. He was so elegant. He was so skilful. He was the best team's best player. John himself, tells a story about two flat-capped old Scousers coming to Anfield to see his home debut and being sceptical about the new signing.

'I'm not sure about this Barnes fella,' one said to the other. 'A black player? Playing for Liverpool? Doesn't seem right.' His companion nodded in agreement as the game kicked off. Ten minutes in, Liverpool won a free kick at the Kop, and Barnes curled the ball into the top corner. The keeper had no chance and Anfield erupted, singing his name and longing for him to once again get on the ball. The old Scouser turned to his mate and said, 'You know what? He's not as black as I thought.'

Thoughts were changing. A black player could be the playmaker, the best player, the most elegant, the one the crowd adore and come to see. There was a grace about John on and off the pitch and I do believe he changed so many perceptions.

Not that football had become this wonderful utopian image of multicultural Britain. There were still places you dreaded going, there were still whispered put-downs on the pitch and slightly louder insults on the terraces. But, going into the 1990s after the World Cup in Italy – all Gazza tears and Pavarotti opera – there did seem to be a gentrification happening in the English game.

After Hillsborough, the Taylor Report had endorsed all-seater stadiums and that was always going to have a positive effect. Some fans say it ruined atmospheres but as a player who got abuse from fans, it changed things, and it further underlined just how cowardly those doing the shouting actually were.

Having to sit down relaxes the idiots. It puts them in a position where they are more noticeable, more alone and they then tend to shout less abuse. Even those who stand in their seats, they're still isolated, there is a space between people and people feel a bit more exposed. There was a new calmness. Did that affect atmospheres? Maybe it did, but the abuse towards so many of us players certainly became less rancid.

Andy's departure to the north-east coincided with a bad run of form for the team, leading to Denis's sacking and the appointment of his assistant, Russell Osman. I liked Russell a lot. First of all, what a footballer, an England international who was so technical. Two-footed, good on the ball, strong in the air, he was a brilliant defender at Ipswich and you sensed that having worked under Bobby Robson there, he was hellbent on playing the game in the right way.

Under Russell, our form picked up and we comfortably avoided relegation (Bristol Rovers went down, which added to our fans' morale) but as the season went on I decided it was to be my last. I had loved playing for Bristol City, I had loved the move west, but you know when it's over. The last game was against Brentford. I scored a hat-trick, Brentford were relegated and I walked away with the match ball. Thank you and goodnight.

There I sat in the dressing room. For so many players, that must be a moment to dread. A funeral-like feeling as the soil of your career is finally thrown on the coffin of your tired body. For me, there was only pure relief that I would no longer be in pain, relief that I no longer had to worry about that knee. Relief and pride. Yes, my career might have been different without the injury, but I had played for far longer than people had expected and at a good level with good players for a good, competitive club. Once again the fans had taken to me and to round things off, I had grabbed a hat-trick. Not bad, Leroy. Not bad at all.

I was also happy to concentrate on coaching. From those early days at Fulham, I had enjoyed the studious part of the game. I liked to learn about the art of being a number nine, and now – having got my coaching badges while injured at West Ham – I looked to pass on that knowledge. Actually, scrap that, it was earlier than those days training with Fulham. I never truly supported a football team, not in the sense that I travelled the country watching matches but I did love to watch and analyse football matches. It's probably why I leant toward coaching and punditry.

> 'I was a defender and so when I was looking for someone, I liked the idea of Leroy, a striker with a natural flair for coaching. I could work on formations and man-management and shape, but to have somebody with knowledge about being a striker, that was great. Leroy was popular and was good for the dressing room so it was an easy decision.'
>
> **Russell Osman, Bristol City manager**

I always watched games differently to proper fans. Then later, so often sitting on QPR's bench, I would study how a game was going. I could often tell there would soon be a chance or a goal, I began to realise an opportunity often stems from two – not one – defensive errors; little things, nuances, but Russell for one saw I had an eye for the game, was a decent communicator and he made me first team coach during my last few months playing.

The summer after my retirement, we went to Wimborne for a pre-season friendly. Luther Blissett had taken over as boss there and it was a good workout for the lads. The thing is I forgot I was no longer one of those lads. We had a tricky and exciting young winger called Junior Bent. On the pitch Junior would have to take a lot of stick. 'Woofing' as I call it. He'd try a trick and get woofed up in the air by a disgruntled defender. As his team-mate, I was always straight over, letting the defender know not to do that again.

At Wimborne, us staff were on the sideline and on the far side, early on, Junior got woofed in the air. I was on, running across the pitch in a coach's tracksuit shouting at the defender responsible, before realising my mistake. I turned around and Russell and all his staff were almost on the floor in hysterics.

Later, Russell asked me to take over the reserves. It felt like a demotion – I presumed it wasn't for my antics in pre-season – but he had his reasons and actually it was good for me. With the reserves there was no pressure. I decided that victory wasn't going to be the be-all and end-all. I had a way I wanted the game to be played so I would encourage constant ball play. If they were in the six-yard box I encouraged my young players to play the ball out. It was a great way to cut my teeth properly.

Not that I wasn't part of first-team affairs as Russell had me working with certain players. Wayne Allison was our centre-forward. A strong, bustling type of goal-getter but for all his strength and power, he couldn't head the ball. Russell took me to one side and asked me to work with him and sure enough, results came. I wasn't exactly using a balloon like I used to do in my parents' living room but the premise was the same, and Wayne began to hang in the air, soon adding headed goals to his impressive repertoire.

Russell kept me very much part of things and in January 1994 that meant being involved in an FA Cup third round tie against Liverpool. Under manager Graeme Souness, Liverpool had struggled to reach the ridiculous heights of the previous decade. They housed plenty of stars though. Ian Rush, John Barnes, Nigel

Clough and a young Robbie Fowler were top players but we felt that they were there to be beaten and maybe we could get at them at our place and cause an upset.

Liverpool came to Ashton Gate and despite their obvious class and an early Rush goal, our lads rallied and started to put pressure on their illustrious guests. Just before half-time we equalised and the fact that it was a Wayne Allison header gave me a certain amount of personal satisfaction.

Unfortunately, the club's floodlights were less illuminated than Allison's new aerial ability and in the second half the game was abandoned due to their untimely failure. So a few days later, Liverpool were back and once again it was Rush who opened the scoring but once again, it was Allison who equalised and so it was a dream trip up to Anfield, one to keep the playing staff and the money men happy.

I travelled up with a buoyant squad and Russell played it brilliantly, laying on a luxury hotel, and treating the tie as if it was the final itself. There is a school of thought that says, don't go to enjoy the experience, go to win, but Russell rightly felt we could do both.

'At Ipswich the club had always made a fuss of the FA Cup, treating it with the respect it deserved. That involved nice hotels, and families coming along too, so I took that on with City. Souness and Liverpool though were first class. Graeme was under pressure but he let us train at their training ground. That was so generous. We went to Melwood and that was special. Our players were used to a few tatty old footballs and suddenly we're on Liverpool's pristine pitches with 40 Adidas Tango footballs pumped up and waiting for us. We went to Anfield feeling on top of the world.'

Russell Osman

We were a buoyant and confident squad, and I had a feeling this would be our night. We enjoyed the pitch and we deserved a 1-0 win, thanks to a Brian Tinnion goal shortly after the hour. Clapped off by the Kop, I was so pleased for the players and for Russell, and I revelled in the buzz a coach can get from the success of his players.

That night we partied hard. Russell had decided we were to stay up on Merseyside whatever the result and we enjoyed a richly deserved five-star night of drink and merriment.

It was over a few drinks in a hotel weeks later that my playing career was unexpectedly and briefly pulled from the comfort of its retirement. Following the Anfield heroics, City had been brought back to earth somewhat with a fourth-round trip to Stockport. Russell and I were sat in the hotel, sharing a few beers and as his team slept, he asked me a question I did not see coming, 'Want to play tomorrow?'

I was still registered and fit, but it had been months since that last game against Brentford. 'How much have you drunk?' I enquired but could see in his eyes that he was serious.

'Fancy a game?'

'Sure.'

With that we went to bed and in the morning I came down for breakfast with a slightly cloudy head. 'Did you ask me to play today, Russell?' I asked, thinking I may have been a bit worse for wear.

'I did and you are.'

Stockport County had a striker called Kevin Francis playing up front, all 6ft 7in of him, and Russell felt me playing at centre-back would nullify his aerial threat. Not that it was a great threat. I had seen Francis play and for his height his leap wasn't up to much and having played plenty of games in defence coaching the reserves, it was felt I could do a job.

'Leroy was still registered and to be honest, he was still the best header of a ball at the club.'

Russell Osman

It wasn't the best of starts. We went out that morning to a local park and worked on set pieces. Defending them, it was agreed that we would – for the first one – all push up and leave them offside. The time came and that's what everyone did…everyone except me, the coach. I totally forgot! A frantic scramble and a quick clearance avoided total disaster but it was an early embarrassment. 'Sorry, boss,' I shouted over to Russell, but from there I got to grips with things and neither Francis nor his team got a look-in. We won 4-0. This time it really was the end though. I had loved playing and showing off my ability and experience, but that was that.

Back home, both my boys were showing talent for the game, but it was Liam (Daron was better built for rugby) who looked from a young age that he would go far. I would tend to watch him play his games from afar. Maybe it was because I was a pro, but I always felt like a distraction rather than a help. Even from behind a tree though, I could see that he had the talent and the football intelligence to go far. My boots might have been hung up, but his were getting ready to play.

10

My Perfect XI

I LOVED being a professional footballer. Training, playing, competing, bettering myself, laughing with team-mates, falling out with team-mates. It was a rich and full time in my life and while I didn't reach the heights in terms of cup finals, league championships and loads of international caps, looking back I did play with some exceptional players and I wanted to underline that point by picking the best XI from those I was fortunate enough to call team-mates.

And what a team it is. A real mix of English, Jamaican, Irish, and Scottish blood. All of them had plenty to say for themselves and while there would be plenty of confrontation and run-ins in their imaginary dressing room, they would always find a way to win. Here's my selection.

Goalkeeper
David Seaman
Football, at any level, can be stressful; training, keeping fit, the pressure of winning, relegation and promotion. Working with David Seaman though, what I remember is walking towards the dressing room and hearing his big, booming laugh and those

pressures seemingly slipping away. That was David. He was so laid-back off the pitch but so assured on it. Everything seemed to be okay when he was around and he took that on from QPR and into his brilliant career at Arsenal and with England.

He was a beast of a goalkeeper. He was still filling out at QPR, but you could just see how far he was going to go. Young keepers can be a bit jittery but David had an old head on his young shoulders. He loved his fishing even then and that summed up his calm personality. Playing in front of him as a defender must have been a joy because of that demeanour of David's. He never screamed at his team-mates – he didn't have to because he used his authority to quietly reassure and organise.

Today so much is made of the goalkeeper's role. They need to be able to use their feet and join in and things like coming and catching the ball seem to have been forgotten. I look at young keepers and they are punching the ball out, but not David. Those big hands would envelop the ball. He never made any save look more difficult than it was and if you asked him to play today, even with this new need to be able to 'play', David would still be England's number one.

Right-back
Paul Parker

Paul was an all-round defender. People forget but he could play centre-half. What was he, 5ft 6in? I remember in training at Fulham once he was marking me and I didn't win a header. Now I was good in the air but on this occasion, Paul leapt and won everything.

I think he played mainly at right-back because of his distribution. He wasn't a bad passer but to play from the back at centre-half it really has to be spot on. Paul could play the channels brilliantly and you never saw him get beaten for speed. He had a fantastic footballing brain, knew the game from a young age and

I remember seeing him when I arrived at Craven Cottage, and you knew, we all knew that this was a future England player.

He also had a calmness. The episode at Leeds where he and I were subjected to Nazi salutes, that affected me badly, but Paul, while I'm sure it hurt, was able to shrug it off. He cared though. They called him 'Arnie' at Fulham after the *Diff'rent Strokes* character and I've said in these pages that I thought he didn't mind. I take that back. I think he did mind but he had the mental strength to deal with it. He will have minded because it undermined him and his incredible ability.

If you ask pros of that era and ask who they think was the best defender they played against, Paul's name will come up. He's certainly the best I ever played with. Fabio Cannavaro captained Italy to the World Cup in 2006 and was similar in build to Paul. Paul was better than him though and that's a massive compliment.

Centre-back
Russell Osman

What a footballer; cultured, plus he had the film star looks to match! At Bristol City we were losing 2-0 and came in for half-time. Russell went nuts at us and read us all the riot act. From the corner of the room came a small voice, 'Come on lads, we can still win this.' It was a homage to the movie *Escape to Victory*, a film Russell was in, and it brought the house down.

There was though so much more to Russell than Hollywood and his looks. If you think of Ipswich's defence in their heyday under Bobby Robson, you think of Terry Butcher and maybe Mick Mills. Look closer and you see how vital Russell was to their slick footballing style. He was a brilliant player.

I got to City and the first thing I noticed was Russell's giant calves. He was a giant of a player who would stick his head in where it hurts but with the ball at his feet he was so slick, so comfortable. I've never seen such a naturally two-footed footballer. The only other one I came across like that from my time was Glenn Hoddle, a player who you couldn't say with any authority whether he was right- or left-footed. Nowadays that simply isn't seen.

He was such a tough character, straight as an arrow and would tell you exactly what he was thinking. That might have got him in trouble but I respected him for that.

Centre-back
Tony Gale

Tony played a major part in my career and I loved playing with him at both Fulham and West Ham. All my team are great company but Tony used to have me crying with laughter. He was always the life and soul of the dressing room. Even today he can just give me a look and I'm laughing.

Tony served his apprenticeship at Fulham under Bobby Moore and it is fitting he had such a brilliant career at West Ham because he was perfect in that centre-back role that required the ability to get on the ball, get your head up and pick a pass.

I've joked that Tony wouldn't go for a 50/50 but in a big melee of players and with the ball in the air, you'd hear 'Tony's ball' and there he'd be pulling the ball down with this great touch and spraying it into a forward's feet. Tony's passes would often make me look good because the ball was so perfectly weighted, it was accommodatingly slowing down as it got to you, making it easy to control.

If anything playing with Tony for so long spoilt me because so often other defenders wouldn't appreciate my runs. He just got that I would make a run away from him to create space before spinning back in to get it to feet. He just got it and I always received the pass where I wanted it.

Today, Tony would make a brilliant holding midfield player, because he had such a great understanding of the game. It is little surprise that a big name like Kenny Dalglish took him to

Blackburn where his valuable experience and that reading of the game helped the team to a Premier League title.

Left-back
Julian Dicks

Think of Julian Dicks and too many of us opt for 'hard man'. Yes, the Bristolian was hard. Very hard in fact, but he was also very good and if it wasn't for those perceptions about his indiscipline I feel he would have won many England caps. Julian was a brilliant striker of the ball. All left foot yes, but he could drive the ball, use the outside of his boot, curl it in, great crosser, good passer, brilliant tackler (and you stayed tackled!) and simply a hard-working pro.

He suffered a horrendous knee injury, ripping his tendons to shreds, but through sheer will and desire to keep playing, he came back and got his big move to Liverpool. That was Julian, very driven and a little bit eccentric. He had pet pigs at West Ham. I'm not sure if they ended up in sandwiches but he was focused on breeding them. He played golf but unlike other footballers this was more than a hobby and he got so good he had a go at the pro game. Always himself, always up for it, that's Julian.

Right midfield
Paul Ince

I'd play a diamond midfield with Paul slightly to the right with a licence to bomb forward. My god, Paul could play. He was up front when I arrived at West Ham but he was at his best driving his team forward from a deeper role. I've never seen a player run with the ball faster than Incey, and while some think of him as a holding midfielder, he was great box-to-box and you only have to look at how he played for England during Euro 96 to see this was an intelligent, brilliant midfielder with an engine that would hurt even world-class opponents.

The thing about Incey was his team ethic. It didn't matter who we played, if they were wearing the opposing kit, he hated them and wanted to crush them. That sounds dramatic but that was Paul Ince. Driven, angry, confrontational, horrible, brilliant. A man who went on to play for Manchester United, Inter Milan and Liverpool. You have to have something about you to play for clubs like that.

In his young days at West Ham he was, for want of a better word, arrogant. That could be great on the pitch as you need that, but off it, sometimes it meant he was misunderstood. For instance after one poor display the fans let us know what they thought of us from outside the team bus and Incey took out a wad of £50 notes and waved them about. Not ideal, but that was him as a young man, totally backing himself and later of course the whole 'Guv'nor' thing was used against him. Get him on his own though and he is a great lad, and one I would so want on my side.

Centre midfield
Stewart Robson

I'd have Stewart at the base of my midfield, not because he was some hard tackling type (although he had that in his game) but he was just so good at reading the game. He was a great footballer. He was a public schoolboy from Essex and when I went to West Ham it was clear he was the driving force, groomed to replace Billy Bonds as the club's captain and talisman.

It was only injury problems that hampered things for Stewart but nevertheless, he was a fine footballer who while frustrated by his career and the problems he faced, should be remembered as a player who could head the ball, pass, run, tackle, nick a goal and lead. Think Steven Gerrard. Stewart might have reached those heights had it not been for his fitness issues.

I like straight people and Stewart was and is. He was a good captain because he had the other players' welfare at heart and would risk falling out with people if he felt things needed to be said. He got sacked by Arsenal TV for consistently criticising Arsene Wenger but he wasn't doing it for the sake of being controversial – he would rather be straight and give his thoughts than toe some sort of party line. It's important that people remember that Stewart was a really, really brilliant player.

Centre midfield
Ray Houghton
Ray would be at the tip of the diamond because he always had a goal in him. A fiery little cracker of a footballer, not the biggest man but a huge character, who always had something to say and would get into bigger men's faces if need be. In that way, he very much symbolised the good Fulham team of the early 1980s.

You don't walk into the Liverpool dressing room of the late 1980s and hold your own (and I hear Ray did) unless you have a strong mentality and of course you have to be able to play. Comfortable in wide positions and brilliantly adept at timing a run into the box, Ray had a great understanding of the game.

What was harder to understand was his accent but this Irish, Glasgow-born, Cockney was a winner in the sense that he would run through walls with the ball and always seem to come out the other side in control of it. I used to laugh because it was like he could read the ricochet. He wasn't a clean dribbler like John Barnes say, but he would get past people. The best way to describe Ray was as a determined dribbler. What he had was this ability to produce real quality – be that a pass, a cross or a shot – while running at pace. Great player, Ray.

Left midfield
Liam Brady
Liam would be on the left but any manager telling Liam to play in only one part of the pitch would need his head examining. Liam

was quality. The best I ever played with for sure and I'd have him playing wherever he wanted. Do what you want, mate.

He was 33 when I got to West Ham, had had the best part of a decade in Italy when Serie A was *the* league to be playing in and he more than held his own. When we talk of the greats to come from Britain or Ireland, Liam has to be in the conversation. Kenny Dalglish, Bobby Charlton, Paul Gascoigne and others, but also Liam Brady.

We used to do two-touch in the boxes at West Ham's training ground and Liam had this ability to dictate play by his brilliance. That sounds weird but he could tell you what to do by the quality of his touch and pass. Like a chess player, he was thinking two moves ahead and only the real greats did that. The ball seemed to talk to you when you linked up with Liam. He was the only player I ever played with who had that ability.

He went into coaching and management but I think he was best suited to working with youngsters and did a great job with Arsenal's youth set-up. I have mentioned in this book that I feel great players should be given well paid, high-profile jobs with youngsters because they are pure footballers and kids have no ego and the likes of Liam would be great at recognising talent.

Striker
Andy Cole

The first time I saw Andy running in training, I was lifted. Coming to the end of my career my move to Bristol City concerned me a bit but all those worries vanished when I saw this gazelle elegantly moving around the training pitch because it meant that I didn't have to.

Quick, single-minded, ambitious, stylish, Andy just had it. He was a magnificent footballer. We both scored on our debuts at City and it was clear that this was a young man going places. He'd shoot from anywhere which got some people's backs up, including mine, until you realised this wasn't Andy being selfish, but just a striker with supreme confidence and the ability to back it up.

It was great working with Andy as a youngster and then, having watched his career from afar and having seen him be so successful, years later I walked into Fulham's players' lounge and there he was sitting with my son, Liam, and I must admit to a small tear in my eye.

Ask the fans who cheered all his goals, just how great a finisher he was and they will have him right up there. Brilliant at Newcastle and then brilliant at Manchester United. At the latter he got a bit of stick for missing chances. Now, that United side was always going to create a lot of chances and no striker scores every one. Only brilliant strikers though get chosen to play for such clubs and Andy was the best I played with.

Striker
Les Ferdinand

Tony Cottee was close to getting in here but I only played a handful of games with him at West Ham and so I'll put Les up top with Andy Cole and what a partnership they'd make. Les came in at QPR from non-league Hayes, very raw, very promising and very nice. It was great when Les arrived at the club because he doubled the black contingent and we clicked immediately.

Les was very driven. After a while with first-team appearances hard to come by, he went to Turkey to play on loan and that underlines just how confident he was and how determined he was to make it because that couldn't have been an easy move but he came back a more complete player and went on to do all the things he did.

He walked back in a man and that's how he played his game, always with his shoulders back and able to boss defences into submission. I see him now, the only black director of football in the game, and I am immensely proud of Les. We need to have role models away from the playing side because playing is a short career and it is vital that black players see Les and what he is doing at QPR and think they can follow.

Manager
John Lyall
It has to be John but he'd be aided by Ray Harford. Both men just knew so much but as a manager, John had everything. He was a teacher, a motivator, a tactician, a father figure. Every day he had an effect on me and taught me and others something new. If you measure others I worked with against John Lyall, no one comes near.

PART THREE

LIAM

11

Pills, Spills and Bellyaches

A LONG queue forms outside a Bristol nightclub. It's the mid-1990s and the thud-thud-thud of the bassline in the club tells you it's a weekend. Revellers waiting to get in move side to side. The girls – dressed in the tiniest of dresses and the strappiest of shoes – have their arms crossed, while the guys – in trousers and shiny, tight shirts – light a cigarette and try to look too hard to fall victim to the night's chill. The movement in the line is nerves. Friday and Saturday night jitters. A nervous excitement caused by the knowledge of impending fun. One by one, they are searched by brawny bouncers with what's left of their body-built necks protruding from their black bomber jackets. People get in, people join. The queue is never ending.

Suddenly a car screeches around the corner and swerves into a space in the club car park. Two guys step out of the car. The passenger is full of bravado. A drink or two has been taken. The driver gets out and the queue starts to murmur. Guys are explaining to their girlfriends. Single girls arch their necks for a closer look. The bouncers give knowing smiles, pull back the velvet rope and let the two men in. No one in the queue complains.

On the side of the parked car are words. It's one of those sponsored cars that once upon a time were enjoyed by football men. Along the side of the car, it reads:

LEROY ROSENIOR – MANAGER OF GLOUCESTER CITY FC

And suddenly you're not a footballer. No regime. No one telling you what time to be somewhere, or what to wear when you get there. My time playing the game was far from the strict existence faced by today's multi-millionaires. Nutritionists were a rare breed back then. One of your five-a-day was the tomato ketchup you had on the fish and chips on the coach back from an away game. Sports science was still screw in-studs on your boots, and away from training and matchday, we were pretty much left to our own devices, as long as it didn't hinder our performance.

That said, the day it dawns on you that you are no longer a professional footballer is a strange one. I've mentioned that I only had feelings of relief about no longer putting my joints on the line but you hear of plenty of horror stories about ex-pros not knowing what to do with themselves. I fear more for Liam's generation.

They live their professional lives being told what to wear, what to eat, when to eat it, what to drink, what not to drink, what girls to avoid in clubs. They have agents on hand to change everything from their employers to their light bulbs. It must be tough to suddenly be told you're out on your own. For me, it was exciting.

I was still coaching at Bristol City so I got that training ground fix that so many pros miss when it's over but I relished the idea of something new. My knee was no longer swollen and in pain and in front of me was nothing but possibility. I knew I wanted to stay in football, and the coaching or even management side of things was appealing but nothing was set in stone, which I liked.

I was also newly single. Of course I would have loved my marriage to have worked but it hadn't and having been married as a teenager I took very nicely to life as a bachelor. Especially in a city like Bristol which is so much smaller than London, but still with a thriving nightlife. I was in my element.

The thing is, if you have played for Bristol City (I can't talk for Rovers players) you are treated like royalty. You're rock stars. There is no real logic for it. It's certainly not based on achievement or the glory you have brought to the city, but you go out, be seen and queues part, drinks are bought, girls flirt and guys swoon. It's incredible and a bit mystifying. Heaven knows what would happen to the place if the club ever won anything.

I embraced that stardom. Why shouldn't I? I lived in a bachelor pad with a mate, Richard, and my friend Martin from London was a frequent visitor and yes, we had fun. Bristol was a very happening city in the 1990s. The country's top DJs would hurry west to play sets in its superclubs such as Lakota. I loved that place. Many a night I would get in there, letting down my hair, no longer hindered by the thought of training, my weight, or indeed a failing marriage.

I became friendly with the guys in local group, Massive Attack. I had plenty of girlfriends (not all at once), I could leave the club at 6am and no one was on hand to mind. It was a brilliantly hedonistic transition from life as a pro to a normal civilian. At one point I even did some work for a local radio station, Galaxy, and actually organised events to compete with BBC Radio 1's roadshows.

It was a strange time but my god, it was fun. I had a bit of disposable cash, but fortunately I wasn't super rich. If I had had the sort of funds that today's footballers will retire on, I would have either blown it all, died, or both. I got a taste of freedom and all the irresponsibilities that seemingly go with it. And one night, maybe I went a bit too far.

My mate invited me back to London and suggested we go to a new club in Elephant and Castle for a night out. The place was Ministry of Sound, relatively new back then but the most popular destination in London's effervescent rave scene. As good a night out as Bristol is, this was on a whole new level. Being Leroy Rosenior wasn't going to get me to the front of this queue but once in, we revelled in the surroundings.

'Here, have this,' my mate said, as we stood by the bar. He dropped a bit of a pill in my mouth, which I gratefully received, and we waited for the debauchery to commence. Half an hour passed and nothing.

'Here, have another bit,' he said.

Another half an hour passed and still nothing. Maybe years as a supreme athlete had rendered my body immune to the powers of class A drugs.

'Here, have another.'

Now after that, time becomes a bit abstract but suffice to say, Martin found me in the club's small cinema room, sitting alone, laughing my head off to a screening of Quentin Tarantino's *Reservoir Dogs*. It was to be my one and only experience of the supposed ecstasy of Ecstasy. As I say, I needed a release after football. I found it, but it was perhaps time for a more solid project.

That came in the unexpected form of Gloucester City Football Club. Tucked away in the Southern League and firmly under a rugby ball-shaped shadow, the club were owned by an ambitious man called Keith Gardiner. Keith had seen me play a lot in Bristol and knew that I had done well coaching both the first team and the reserves.

When asked to take over and become manager, I immediately agreed. Technically I was going to be player-manager but the former never interested me. It was getting my coaching ideas into practice and testing them in a competitive league that got my juices flowing but first I'd have to win over the players. I was, after all, the boss.

I had been interviewed for the role, but arrived in the nearby TGI Fridays restaurant having done my homework and I set about being interviewed but also interviewing Keith. I had looked at the squad and seen the quality was there but I also wanted to know how ambitious the club were and what sort of funds were available.

Keith, a slick salesman (he won't mind me calling him that), was clearly a man of ambition and the regularity with which he opened his chequebook allowed me to build a formidable team. My front line was the talk of the division and their play matched the hype. David Holmes, Dale Watkins and Ade Mings were fantastic for me. They were big players at that level, the latter being an absolute beast of a goalscorer.

* * * * *

I loved it. I was on £25,000 a year, had a sponsored Renault Laguna and was brimming with ideas. The hardest thing would be time as I had too much of it on my hands. Tuesday and Thursday nights were training and Saturdays were matchdays. I would fill my hours doing more prep than most professional managers but the fact is, there were times when I got bored. Being used to the day-to-day buzz of a football club, I wasn't ready for the part-time game, but no matter, that was my new life and as I say, working with the players was more than making up for my lack of time with them.

That's the great thing about non-league and the part-time element of it. The passion of those you work with. I've sat in professional dressing rooms and thought that if I was the manager I would question certain players' work ethic or desire to put in the hard graft. The guys I started managing at Gloucester had more passion for the game than I had ever seen. They would wake up at seven, go and do their jobs, pack the kit that they had washed and the boots they had lovingly polished and come to training and once there, they would – and this is the basic any coach wishes for – listen.

I had a way I wanted to do things at Gloucester and every single player I had there bought into it. You can't ask for more than that as a manager. If you don't have that, you are struggling. The players – most of them already good enough to be professionals – listened, took it on board and we were that year, in my biased but educated opinion, the best team in the division.

I got such a buzz (better than any pill!) from watching players learn in training and put what I had worked on into practice on a Saturday. We weren't only winning games but we were winning in style. We had around 2,500 passionate fans coming to watch us and enjoy a winning team, something they hadn't really seen before.

That's another huge plus about non-league football. The link between playing staff, manager and the supporters is crucial and unlike anything you find in the pro game. The fans want more than to just watch and support. There must be a link, a relationship. Beers are shared after games, as are honest opinions. The fans are almost the boardroom you answer to and I loved that. I love talking about football, love dissecting a match and so to start off my coaching career at a level where I could do that with passionate fans was a joy.

We were never going to compete with rugby in the city but my bosses could see immediately that we'd created a buzz around the football ground and maybe, just maybe, promotion one day to the Football League was on the cards. One thing that had never even come up since I joined the club was the colour of my skin. Football being football though, it soon would.

We travelled for a pre-season friendly and after the game I went upstairs for the required post-match formalities with my chairman and the opposition's board. I approached the door, only to be stopped by an officious doorman, dressed head to toe in the finest regalia, and adamant that I couldn't be the manager of Gloucester City.

I remonstrated for a while but this very important gentleman was having none of it. As if guarding the crown jewels themselves, he stood steadfast until I took matters into my own hands and dialled my chairman on my new mobile phone. Keith came out of the room, asked what all the fuss was about and confirmed that I was in fact the man I said I was.

'Oh, sorry sir,' the official said. 'Do come in.'

'Shove your boardroom up your arse,' came my curt response.

Keith was more shocked than me. My colour, in his eyes, had never even come into it. Being black wasn't going to hinder or benefit the job he wanted me to do but in the game itself, it was a factor. Black coaches and managers were very rare, almost unheard of in fact and so starting out, this time with a tracksuit on, suddenly felt a bit like running out and playing as a teenager in the early 1980s.

This time though, my skin was thick as well as black, and the only thing keeping me awake at night was my football club. Luckily, I slept very well as we continued to win games and impress with a brand of football I had always envisaged playing. I had the team playing 3-4-3, then 3-5-2, then 4-4-2, always adapting. We were quick and strong but we trusted each other and the ball was always on the deck. If anything, our winning formula would turn out to be our downfall.

We had gone on this long run in the FA Trophy. It had started with a game against Kingstonian in which I had to fulfil the player part of my role as player-manager but on this occasion I was in goal. Our regular keeper, David Coles, had got injured late in the day, so I volunteered. I had no qualms about doing so. You have to be brave to go in goal and I enjoyed timing my leap, punching the ball away, throwing myself at people's feet. Maybe it was my old wicket-keeper days playing cricket as a kid that helped me, but I did okay. We won 3-1 and their goal was a penalty.

The run went on and on and we were missing key games in the league. Cheltenham Town would run away with the league but there was that runners-up spot and despite having to play seven games in 12 days, win our last and a place in the Conference was ours. I'll never forget that day.

Nearly 3,000 people came to our little Meadow Park stadium for a final game against Salisbury FC. Helicopters buzzed overhead. For one afternoon, with pro football close enough to touch, rugby played second fiddle in the city. I absolutely loved giving my team-talk that day. I was so proud of my team of part-timers but one more push, one last 90 minutes and they could make history.

Things got very raucous as we went one up, but as the game progressed I could sense that it was going to be very hard. I had long watched games of football and I had long tested myself against the country's best, and standing in the dugout, I saw, probably even before my players felt it, that legs were going. There was a gradual lethargy, not visible to the fans who roared them on, but I knew. The legs – these part-time legs that had given so much over the season and worked so hard over the last fortnight of it – could give no more. We lost 3-1.

Talk about heartbreak. To see my players come so close and to fall at the last desperate hurdle, I'd say that was the biggest blow in my career. Sure, it wasn't the FA Cup, the Milk Cup or the First Division, but I had worked with these guys and to coach them and then see the pain in their eyes, that was tough.

Saying that, what a night out we had afterwards. We all dusted ourselves off and joined our fans in a local club where booze and tears flowed in equal measure. I remember my big centre-half, a talented footballer called Gary Kemp, who would go from downing shots with me to weeping on my shoulder. 'We let you down boss,' he'd say. 'Right at the end, we let you down.'

He couldn't have been more wrong. I reassured him and we enjoyed what was one of the best nights out of my life.

Working with the likes of Gary was so rewarding. Here was this big, part-time centre-half. Brilliant defensively, powerful, good in the air but I knew if I wanted the team to play a passing game, my centre-halves needed to be able to play. I gave Gary the confidence in his own ability. I only coached him on Tuesday and Thursday evenings but to see him take on board what I was saying, watch him, aged 27, get on the ball, move it out with the outside of his foot, line up a pass; that was as rewarding as coaching any young pro.

It had been a great ride. Being the manager of Gloucester brought so much. Experience, a taste of how passionate football can be, something you can forget working in the pro game, groupies, the confidence to know I could do this at a higher level and a tremendous amount of fun. Yes, I did say groupies. I was single and kudos could be found, even as boss of Gloucester. In fact I went out with a girl I met at Meadow Park for two years.

The club though was still non-league, and as it turned out that was probably for the best. Keith was so ambitious, so keen to get promotion that he had gambled a lot of money on success and the club were actually going bust. On our FA Trophy run to the semi-final, the team played away at Bishop's Stortford, in Hertfordshire, and we stayed at a luxury hotel, which we shared with Chelsea. Now, they stayed for the one night, but little Gloucester stayed for two.

Keith paid the £6,000 hotel costs with his credit card. Weeks later that bill still hadn't been paid, his credit clearly unable to match the hotel's demands. Things were going wrong. Even if we had gone up, there is no way the club could have survived as a professional outfit. Not that I was going to bail out. It would be hard but there was still work to be done.

Firstly we had to sell our best players. Ade Mings, Dale Watkins, David Holmes, my brilliant front line, they all had to go. For the next year or so, things would be tough on the football pitch. We finished around 12th I think but it was a case of looking after the pros I had and the players I had grown fond of. Becoming mates with your players isn't always seen as the managerial thing to do, but that's what had happened with my part-time guys. I respected them so much and I was going to work hard to make sure that they were paid and their contracts were honoured.

The excitement of that first campaign had been dampened by economics so it wasn't a hard decision when Bristol City came to me with a job offer. To be assistant academy director in my early 30s was an exciting prospect but I also wanted to be closer to the boys. Liam was at Bristol Rovers and doing well but I wanted him with me at City where the set-up was that much better, more professional.

I would be in charge of the kids aged eight to 16. Russell Osman was looking after the 18s to 21s and we worked under David Burnside, the head of the academy and a former FA man, who I struggled to get on with. He was a stickler for detail. Everything had to be signed off. We were in at 7am and the place felt very regimented. I loved coaching and working with youngsters but the actual environment wasn't ideal. I found myself getting frustrated at the level of paperwork, meetings and frankly anal detail required by David. I wanted to be coaching more than I was, and every little thing that took me off the pitch, grated with me, leaving me feeling slightly suffocated.

I would often be taking a session and David or his assistant, Peter Amos, would come over and say, 'Okay, that's enough, come in.' But that wasn't enough, I hadn't finished my session but there was a meeting to get to. I wasn't one to hide my frustrations and at times, relations with David were stretched.

At Bristol, we had a talented kid called Marvin Brown. David went public and announced he was going to be the first £10m player. It was a ridiculous statement. Sure, Marvin had a lot of promise and was playing under-19 football for England but to put that sort of pressure on a young man was wrong. I sensed there was politics at play and David had gone public in order to boost only his and the academy's reputation. Sod the kid's progress. It was another sticking point with me as I started to realise that so much in the game goes on away from footballs and goalposts, and you better get used to it.

He did offer me some nuggets of information though. Firstly he always said, you can't make a chicken salad with chicken shit, a saying that stuck with me and alluded to the fact that you shouldn't waste time with bad players. He also underlined the importance of not being a prisoner to your own experience.

Many coaches and managers are too quick to judge a player or a situation by what they went through, forgetting that individuals are just that. The game might have moved on and it's vital you put yourselves in the players' boots. Many top players struggle in management for those reasons, finding it hard to relate to lesser players but also relying only on their own experiences to try and solve a problem.

It was an intense time. I would coach all week, get David's paperwork done and the weekend was games. For 11 months I coached, I did games, over and over. It was an amazing learning curve, the most educational time in my career.

'A coach has to earn respect but you have to be able to deal with people and that's the same whether you're working with kids, senior pros or senior pros on a lot of money. They have to look at the coach and think, this guy knows what

he is on about. That is the stature Leroy had. Whether he
was with the under-14s or Andy Cole in the first team, he
had a way about him. For me, he never talked up or down
to anyone and that is key in this crazy game.'

Russell Osman

Working with kids was so rewarding and taught me a lot and
every two years when the England team fail and the same debate
rages about what is wrong with the national team and the calibre
of player we produce, I am reminded about an argument I once
had with David at Bristol's academy.

The problem is club's youth coaches are seen by far too many
people as also-rans. They are offered tiny salaries, often too little
to survive on and treated as second class citizens. The best former
players and the best coaches need to be with the youth team players
and that should be seen as one of, if not, *the* best job. If you value
youth development, the best people should be with them.

Look at Holland. Dennis Bergkamp works with 11-year-olds.
In England it is old grandpa Bill or old uncle Frank. No offence
to either of them but these plucky volunteers on £3 an hour aren't
going to give you the best players.

Being England manager is a hard job, but it should just
be a figurehead, a frontman who deals with the pressures of
tournament football and the press. The team doesn't need the
best coach, they are established footballers. The best coach
available should look after youth development. They should be
given a healthy salary, a five-year contract and be told to work
and produce. They should work and feel valued because in this
country, youth team coaches just aren't.

The Bristol City manager's office had been worked hard since
Russell left the main job in November 1994. Joe Jordan, John
Ward, Benny Lennartsson, Tony Pulis; they'd all had brief reigns
so in 2000, I had a chance to work closely with the first team.

Myself, David Burnside and Tony Fawthrop became a caretaking triumvirate. It was an exciting prospect but of course already stretched relationships were going to prove hard to overcome. The three of us had a meeting and David and Tony suggested that I do the media stuff. I had done local TV and it was felt I was good with the press, so I'd be the frontman with them. Fine by me. Coaching schedules were shared and we went on a long unbeaten run, even getting to the Football League Trophy Final, and all seemed hunky dory.

One day, I got to work and David called me into his office. With a serious look on his face he suggested that we should share the media responsibilities. I was confused but the penny soon dropped. They thought I was getting too much exposure, maybe getting the credit for the team's success. I had only done what was asked. More politics.

It was a frustrating time. The three managers wasn't going to work long-term but I was hopeful of actually getting the job full-time. Instead Tony got it. I was gutted. Tony had never done a coaching badge, let alone played the game. He was a fixer, a handyman around the club and so to be overlooked was a blow.

I had played for the club, was popular among the supporters, had my badges, knew the local press well, knew the academy like the back of my hand, but instead I was being asked to step back. I was fuming. It was an eye-opener. You can't help but analyse things after that sort of rejection and I couldn't help but wonder, if I had been a white former player who knew so much about the football club, would I have got the job? I'm afraid to say the answer seemed to me, a resounding yes.

As it turned out, Tony was involved in a business scandal and didn't last long in the job, just a matter of weeks in fact. Once again I didn't get the job, but this time it was easier to take as I missed out to Danny Wilson, a proper football man, who was clearly qualified for the position.

Danny came in and asked me to put a session on with the first team. I knew it was a test but I revelled in it and the players responded well. From there, Danny and I got on well. He was a great manager and I learnt so much from him in the short time we worked together.

I though, had itchy feet and with hindsight, began to go through the motions somewhat. The quality of my work never dipped, but my mind was elsewhere, in a manager's office, my own manager's office. I was desperate to move on and get my own job somewhere but while I had first-team sessions to sort, youth team games to get to, and academy politics to navigate, I wasn't putting enough energy into realising those ambitions. I needed change to happen and football being football, soon a good old-fashioned falling-out would open up new career paths.

12

No Matter What I Do

LONDONERS have long enjoyed travelling west to Devon. The glitterati of Victorian society liked nothing more than boarding a steam train and escaping the smog of the capital for the cleaner air of what they now called the English Riviera.

During the Second World War, Cockney kids waved goodbye to their rubbled homes and weary parents, and headed that way to escape the Luftwaffe's nightly visits, for a county where the skyline was infinitely more friendly. Even Sherlock Holmes packed his pipe and deer stalker hat and made his way from Baker Street to Dartmoor where supposedly, a hound was terrorising those poor Baskervilles.

Perhaps that's why, as I drove through Newton Abbot towards my new home, I felt so at ease. I'd never felt that sort of connection before. Being a footballer you live a nomadic sort of life but as I approached Torquay, it was like driving back to Thornbury Road in Brixton; familiar, friendly, strangely just like home.

I knew I could do good things here. Don't ask me why, but it was a positivity that had been missing from my working life for a while. I loved the academy at Bristol City but it had got unbearably political and my working relationships had all but collapsed around me.

Chairman John Layock and academy director Pete Amos weren't my sort of people. We didn't see eye to eye and it reached boiling point one day when a simple request involving Liam blew up in my face.

I had a first team game to be at in the afternoon and having watched Liam play that morning for the youth side, I asked if he could be excused the warm-down as I needed to rush off. Not the most controversial of requests but it created a huge bust-up. The coaches got upset with Liam, Liam got upset with the coaches, and incredibly, I was hauled up in front of a disciplinary panel and it was eventually decided I should leave the club by mutual consent.

The whole thing left a bitter taste in my mouth, which is a shame because I loved City and to this day feel a closeness and warmth to the place, but no matter how much a club gets under your skin, it is individuals and your relationships with them that count. There was obvious politics at foot, and my sour relationship with Laycock – we simply didn't like each other – and others at the club such as Amos, meant my being there wasn't feasible.

From Bristol, in March 2002 I took a temporary job at Merthyr Tydfil in the Southern League. They were threatened with relegation and I went in hoping to turn it around. I didn't. No disrespect, but the team were mostly local lads, honest players but lacking quality and I tried too much for such a short time in charge. I brought in a load of new players but, rather than too little too late, perhaps it was too much, too late.

So I had some time to myself. What would I do next? The answer was some decking in the garden and it was while out there, varnishing the new woodwork, that the phone went. It was Mike Bateson, the chairman of Torquay Football Club. 'I've been expecting you to call me, Leroy,' he said, sounding rather like an evil villain from a Bond film.

Months earlier, while at Bristol City, I had gone for the manager's job at Torquay, but missed out to Roy McFarland. No argument. Roy was an ex-England international and experienced manager. I had enjoyed the whole interview process though and felt I had given a good account of myself. At the time, Mike had said he was impressed and that I had run Roy a close second, but like a jilted teenage lover, I presumed he said that to all the guys. Turns out he didn't.

'You've read that Roy, has left us, right?' Mike asked.

'Yeah, of course.'

'Well, I thought you'd call to ask for the job?'

'Well, I'll ask now. Can I have the job?'

'Yes.'

With that I was a Football League manager. Going over the finer details was a simple process, which is exactly the way I wanted it. Mike and I had further talks and I made sure that it was easy to appoint me. No big demands, no big diva requests. In terms of payment and contracts, I accepted incentives. Do well and a contract would be available. I backed myself. I had done it at Gloucester, and I knew I could do it here.

I was confident, but I was also a realist. The club were getting 2,500 people through the turnstiles and this is a remote part of England's footballing map. What I had was the will, the drive and the energy to put in the work needed. I was young, I was single. Why not? I could see the bigger picture and have always been – be it as a player, a coach, a manager and now a pundit – of the thought that if you put in the hard work, good things will come your way.

So it was time to get started. Norman Medhurst, the former England physio and all-round great bloke, was at the club and was the perfect companion. My legs were at last under the desk in a Football League manager's office, and now it was time to get down to work. I say office. At training – in the middle of Newton

Abbot racecourse – while the players got changed in the allocated hut, I would sit in the chairman's Range Rover.

I'm sure the players must have seen us sitting there, and thought we were plotting club policy, transfer strategy or maybe Saturday's tactics. We weren't. He was telling me crap jokes and I was telling him crap jokes. It was all very relaxed but summed up just how confident and settled I felt starting out at the club.

For one, I knew my squad. Working at the academy and then managing at non-league level with Gloucester, I had a good knowledge of West Country football and was more than aware of the players in the bottom tier of the Football League and so I knew that I was working with decent footballers. I wouldn't have taken the job otherwise. Not with the tiny budget I had.

David Graham was a fantastic attacker, and the likes of Alex Russell and Jason Fowler I knew very well. These guys were key. I had to get them onside from the off as they were the heartbeat of the club. I have mentioned how, at QPR, Terry Fenwick ran the place, well at Torquay these guys – in a far less authoritarian way – were that heartbeat. Get them believing in me and my methods and the job was half done.

What was great about the chairman was that any funds from gate receipts went straight back into the team. David was a great attacker but I realised I needed more goals and so went on the hunt, trying to track down Jo Kuffour, a youngster who had won the FA Youth Cup with Arsenal but seemed to have disappeared.

Time to call Derry Quigley, my old mate and mentor from Fulham. A kind of footballing Batman, who knew everyone in and everything about the game in London. The capital was his Gotham City and in a matter of days he had tracked down Jo and we persuaded him to pack his things and head west.

'I'd left Arsenal and wondered what my next move was. Derry must have got hold of my agent because it was him who came to me and said Torquay were keen. ITV Digital had gone bust which affected the money in the Football League. It was said I could just go to Torquay to train, but after a few days with Leroy, I realised this might be the right place to play permanently.'

Jo Kuffour, Torquay player

With Jo up front and scoring I had moved David to a wider position but before a game against Exeter, he came to me with a suggestion, 'Boss, I think I should be playing up front where Jo is.' It was a bold statement but David was a confident lad and as I listened to his measured argument, I decided to grant his wish. He'd play up front with Jo.

Now, the Exeter game is the biggest of the season, a West Country derby that might mean nothing to the game's elite but means everything in Devon. I listened and I agreed because David coming to me was exactly the environment I wanted to nurture. I had no coaching staff, so I wanted dialogue between myself and the players. I wanted honesty and openness between us all.

I believed that David would be better wide on this occasion but I saw in his eyes that he wanted it, and had I listened and then merely said, 'Thanks but no thanks,' he'd have never come to me again. Instead, he scored twice in a 3-1 win.

My methods were working. The excitement I took with me on to the training pitch seemed to be infectious with the players and they immediately bought into me and what I wanted from them. My plans, my sessions, my players, my team. This was the Football League and I was loving it.

I wanted Torquay to be all about possession. Every warm-up in training was technical and with the ball. Inside of the foot, outside of the foot, chest, little volleys, always with the football. Small games, keep ball, rotation. Rotation of movement and rotation of midfield players. Players love working with the football and I could see the enthusiasm they all immediately had for what we were doing was going to transfer to matchday.

> 'Training was so fun. You think lower league and you think long ball, but I was up front and I'm no big man so everything was along the floor. That was key for me. I had been brought up at Arsenal when everything revolved around total football. I didn't expect to get that again as I dropped down the leagues, but at Torquay with Leroy, I was so pleasantly surprised because the sessions were so similar to what I had experienced with Arsene Wenger. Not much running, small-sided games, technical stuff.'
>
> *Jo Kuffour*

I used David Graham as a nine and a half, allowing him to drop into areas that opponents didn't like. The key was possession but I didn't want my team to overpass. We wanted to be direct but with the ball at our feet. I wanted direct running and I drummed into my forwards to never miss an opportunity to turn and run at defenders; cue runners from midfield to get beyond them and hopefully wreak havoc. Often, teams just couldn't cope.

Away from home, we used that possession to manage a match. Okay, so it's not a European super club travelling abroad and shutting up a hostile crowd, but it was the same principle. We would go and keep the ball for 15 minutes. It looked like we were taking the piss, and sometimes, I guess we were.

From the dugout, I could hear fans, all over the country, in big northern or Midlands towns, saying, 'Fuckin' hell, it's only Torquay!' That got my back up. It was almost disrespectful so I'd fold my arms and revel in my team passing the ball around their supposed sleeping giants. We wore the yellow shirts and the blue shorts and I'd love how it was like watching Brazil. Little

Torquay from the Riviera, little Torquay from the land of scones and clotted cream. Little Torquay humiliating your team.

We surprised a lot of people. On one occasion those people happened to be the best striker in the country. We went to Hartlepool who were managed by Mike Newell. In the stands was Alan Shearer, an old mate of Newell's from Blackburn and resident/legend of the north-east. That was one of my favourite games. We lost 3-2 to a very good side but we passed and we passed and it was end to end. A thrilling advert for the bottom tier of our game. Afterwards, Shearer said that that was the best game he'd seen all season. He couldn't believe the quality on show.

With Shearer's endorsement in my ears, that was a good coach journey home, but being Torquay, it was a long one. They all were. I loved them though. As a player I had always enjoyed the bus rides involved, and with this bunch, the camaraderie and the jokes made the endless stretch of English motorway more than bearable. For some reason, we were always listening to RnB's Nelly and Kelly from Destiny's Child. Their track 'No Matter What I Do' (an apt title for us black coaches!) was always on and I can't listen to it today without smiling and thinking of happy times.

> *'No matter what I do*
> *All I think about is you*
> *Even when I'm with my boo*
> *You know I'm crazy over you'*

That game at Hartlepool was symptomatic of my team. We were brilliant with the ball but going into the 2003/04 season, I knew we had been too soft, we needed to be sterner without the ball. That's why we had come ninth. Mike had set me no targets but I was sure this team could mount a challenge for promotion, or the play-offs at least so we delved into the transfer market. I say delved, we went on the hunt for loans and the game's waifs and strays.

Fortunately, nearby Plymouth were doing brilliantly under Paul Sturrock. I had a great relationship with Paul and he would loan me players, knowing they'd be playing good football with us. I got Craig Taylor – a good, strong centre-back – from them as he'd been released. I took a young local lad called Matt Hockley who didn't look like a footballer but what an attitude. I had previously played with two ball-playing midfielders in Jason Fowler and Alex Russell but we needed a ball winner. Matt sat in, tackled anything in a 30-yard radius, and gave it simple to Jason or Alex. I had Tony Bedeau, a great winger, and Kevin Hill, only five feet something but brilliant in the air. I remember, he used to crouch at corners. Crouch to make himself even smaller and then leap and win everything.

I was loving it. Planning sessions, seeing them executed, watching players improve. This was fantastic. I was the boss. Not that I was one for screaming and ranting. I had played under the likes of Jim Smith who could reduce a dressing room to rubble with his bollockings but I was of calmer stock. I had worked only six months with Danny Wilson at City but I had learnt that losing your temper as a manager was plain stupid. Danny taught me that if you are going to scream and shout, do it with purpose, do it to get a reaction, but only if you feel a player or the team need it. The proof is in the word lose. If you lose your temper, you've lost something. That may sound a bit like middle management lingo but it's true.

> 'With Leroy, it was more the face. He wasn't one to throw things around the dressing room but he had this expression, this look on his face. He'd walk in, with pursed lips and these wide eyes. You'd get your head down and look at your boots and listen. That look. It was like when your mum says, "I'm not angry, I'm disappointed."'
>
> *Jo Kuffour*

Anyway, what did I have to lose my temper about? Life was sweet. In 2003, I met Luci. My old mate Martin and I were making fools of ourselves in a club in Exeter, and Luci, who was doing her teaching qualification at Exeter University, tolerated me and agreed to meet me again.

Before my second season at Torquay, as I was adding to my team, I realised I needed a bit of quality and thought of Liam. Bristol City had failed to offer him a contract and so with the help of a £55,000 compensation fee, Fulham had taken him on and he was working hard to get into their Premier League first team. I had a player who could call me Dad as well as Boss.

My motives though were purely professional. With Liam I knew I was getting a player with the right attitude, he was far from big time. I needed versatility and Liam could play right-back, centre and right side of midfield. I also knew the players would like him. Liam is no daddy's boy.

It might take a few weeks but any reservations his team-mates might have wouldn't last.

> 'I had got an unbelievable move to Fulham but needed some first team football and so Torquay it was. I moved in with him on the understanding that at work he was the boss and at home I was the boss!'
>
> *Liam Rosenior*

When he first arrived, you wouldn't have blamed the players for wondering if this was nepotism gone mad. The drills we always did, Liam just couldn't get used to. It wasn't that he wasn't good enough but he wasn't used to them. I knew he would pick them up but I could see the team's collective eyebrows were raised.

The worry for me was that Liam was a bit blasé about them, a bit nonplussed but like my team, I knew these drills were vital for how we played, technical and quick. Every little pass, every little volleyed pass, everything had to be on the money, otherwise possession was given up and that was sacrosanct.

> 'Dad and I had driven in together as usual. We wouldn't talk about football, just life, like any father and son. Then we get to training and Norman comes to me and says, "The boss wants to talk to you." I'm thinking, he's just had breakfast and driven in with me. I go to see him and he says, "I'm dropping you today, you look tired." I couldn't believe it. I was sub. He had had the whole morning to tell me but it's at work, where he's boss, that he drops his bombshell.'
>
> *Liam Rosenior*

Now that caused a stir. I wanted the team to know that Liam was there to play, that on matchday he was exactly the same as them. I wanted to reiterate to Liam that he hadn't trained well and being the fruit of my loins wasn't going to make that acceptable. After 20 minutes we were two down, Liam was sent on and we drew 2-2.

I had bought a converted church between Torquay and Exeter which Liam moved into with me. Having been dropped, he didn't speak to me for three days. Aged 19, this was the last of his teenage sulks but it was a whopper.

> 'I stared out of the window, the whole drive home. I didn't want to look at him or talk to him. Proper teenage stuff. What made it worse was my brother Daron came down, walked in and said, "Liam, you're so bad, even your own dad won't pick you." My little brother! I wanted to kill them both.'
>
> *Liam Rosenior*

I took the silent treatment and from there, Liam adapted to our methods and was superb for the team. Family feuds sorted, what followed was a season that gave me the most pleasure in my career. The new additions were perfect and while allowing us to play the same, smooth, possession-based football, we were no longer a soft touch.

> 'We were brilliant. If you look more recently at what the likes of Roberto Martinez did at Swansea or Eddie Howe at Bournemouth, this was the same. Under dad we were playing the same slick football and he didn't have a penny to spend. The key was fun. Football can be too serious. You can't achieve things in football, especially on such a low budget, without having a smile on your face, and I was proud of my dad for making that time at Torquay so memorable, whilst at the same time, making the players better.'
>
> *Liam Rosenior*

The play-offs looked our most likely shot at promotion, and Mike had booked a cruise. Going into the last weekend there was a chance of an automatic spot but it meant Huddersfield needing to drop points at Cheltenham and for us to win at Southend. Mike decided to go on his cruise and be back for the play-offs. Fine.

Weeks earlier, we had gone to Cheltenham and beaten them 3-1. That was the best. We were brilliant. Jo and David received standing ovations from the Cheltenham fans, John Ward – the Cheltenham boss – said we were the best team they had faced, and we went home feeling good about ourselves but perhaps a little frustrated that we would probably have to contend with the play-offs. So, on a balmy May day, we went from our seaside to Southend's and were followed by thousands of Torquay fans, far more than we usually got at our home games. What followed was a surreal afternoon. We played slightly nervously but were 2-1 up and it was ears to transistor radios (the chairman, from the comfort of the cabin of his cruise liner, was doing just the same). Huddersfield were 1-0. No change. Play-offs here we come.

I had a defender called Reuben Hazell, who was good but a little rash. Southend broke in the box and Reuben lunged, the player went down and it was a nailed-on penalty. The ref said play on. Norman and I looked at each other and laughed. Maybe something was in the stars.

Suddenly, I sensed a stirring from our lot behind the goal, a murmur than turned into a roar, and I looked behind me for news. Cheltenham had equalised and if it stayed like that, we were up. There were only minutes left but it seemed a lifetime.

There is nothing you can do in that situation. You scream at players to work, keep a shape, move their legs, knowing as a former pro that in the 92nd minute those legs won't do as they're told. This is life as a fan or a manager. You want it so much but you can only watch, scream and pray.

The final whistle blew but we had to wait a few minutes for news from Cheltenham. It was agonising. We waited for longer and then came the news. They'd done it for us!

Fans of bigger clubs might chuckle at the level of celebration a team like Torquay might put into coming third in the Third Division (as it was then) but when you work so hard this is no different to winning the Champions League. In fact to bring success to a club that size where money wasn't either an aid or the incentive was the best feeling.

The players went crazy, myself and Norman went crazy, the directors loosened their ties and went crazy, Dave Thomas, the local journalist who travelled with us everywhere went crazy, and the fans, those intrepid souls who cross the nation to watch us, went beyond crazy.

This being Torquay, we had no refreshments so the coach pulled over on the way home at a Tesco and the directors opened their wallets and stocked up on booze and we partied all the way home. I sat, drank, sang, laughed and wallowed in what we had all done and the great thing about that day was that I did it all with my son. I don't keep many pictures of my career but I cherish the one of Liam and myself embracing after the game.

The club had taken a step up for the first time since 1991. We had an open-top bus ride through the streets of the town as the feelgood factor rolled in off the English Channel. The club's stock was up and so was mine. In the next season I was approached by Brighton in the First Division. It was a big job, at a club who had plans. They were still playing at the temporary and far from ideal Withdean Stadium but the chairman, Dick Knight, met me and once again I made a good account of myself in the interview, losing out to Mark McGhee who had recently managed Celtic and had won caps for Scotland.

I went back to Torquay, gutted to have missed out but that's football. The following week we lost 4-0 at Boston United, and I realised I had lost focus on the job at hand and it was going to be hard enough up a division (what with increased crowds and extra costs, promotion actually cost the club money) without me taking my eye off the ball.

Once again, we had boxed clever in the transfer market and I had gone looking for a striker I knew to be good, but who had lost his way. This time Adebayo Akinfenwa, who later became a cult figure at AFC Wimbledon, had, like Jo Kuffour, disappeared but once again we tracked him down and got him. I liked him a lot. Great player. Good feet. Great in the air. Strong. Very big but it was muscle, not fat, and very keen. Very quick. Oh, and he was free.

He was a bit of a loose cannon, he could go missing but the talent was there. I – like Ray Harford and Derry had done with me so many years before at Fulham – taught him to get side-on and he did very well for us.

His goals though weren't going to save us from a hard season. It was always going to be hard but we had a chance to survive right up to the end, winning four games in a row in April, but still we had to win our last game. Once again it was a trip to Essex for that final, decisive match but this was Colchester and unlike Southend 12 months earlier, there was to be no jolly by the sea. We left Colchester defeated and relegated and that was so hard to take.

Football, like life, throws success and failure at you in often equal measure but despite Rudyard Kipling's musings, I struggled to deal with the latter. Relegation took the wind firmly from my sails and it felt like all the energy that had made the job both enjoyable and successful had gone. My chairman Mike saw it and suggested I use the break to recharge myself, and I hoped he was right.

Luci and I had by now moved into an idyllic cottage on the coast near Torquay and that year had Millie, my daughter. We could walk her on the beach and in so many ways life was fantastic. It was professionally that I felt I was having to force things and in football, if you are having to force things, players know and you begin to lose them.

I started the following season at Torquay but a run of poor form matched my continued apathy for the work, and in January 2006, I left by mutual consent. It was a hard job, club and town to leave. Not once in that last year did one fan ever get on my back. I think they had – as much as the players – bought into what I was doing and enjoyed the fun ride that we had been on together. I walked out, my head held high.

Liam had gone back to Fulham where he had broken into the first team, had captained the club and was on his way to a brilliant career. For his old man, the future was less clear. Sherlock Holmes might have come to Devon and cracked the Baskerville mystery but while I felt I had taken small steps in cracking the mystery of management, this was no time to sit back and smoke my pipe. Football, after all, is far from elementary.

13

No More Mr Nice Guy

'YOU'RE too nice.' Greg Dyke, the Brentford chairman, has sacked me and in a room full of directors has given his reason. 'It's not worked out, Leroy. Maybe you're too nice.' Too nice? I felt like smashing his face in. *How nice is that, Greg?*

I had only been at the west London club for four months, but we had been on a dreadful run of form. I expected to be sacked, that's football, time is a luxury most managers seldom enjoy, but too nice? My fists clenched, as did my jaw. *'Keep your powder dry, son.'* I thanked Greg and the directors for the opportunity, and I walked out.

After Torquay, I had wanted to get back in the game as soon as possible. The phone wasn't ringing but there was no way I was just going to sit around sulking and waiting. Football won't allow that. Gary Peters was at Shrewsbury Town and midway through the season, he needed a new assistant. A coach with different ideas.

Was it a step down? Technically yes, but I didn't think of it that way. You have to duck and dive in football. I am a firm believer in work. Work somewhere and work hard. Do that, and opportunity will come your way. That's what I did and I thoroughly enjoyed my time with Gary. We didn't quite make the play-offs but I was on the training pitch every day working with decent footballers, and that was enough. For now.

It was agreed that I would only see the season out at Shrewsbury, and, that summer, I took a phone call from my old mentor Derry Quigley. He had been in touch with another London scout, John Griffin, who had the ear of the Brentford board. They had recently parted ways with their manager Martin Allen and wanted a new style of play, a manager who could develop their young players and having seen Torquay winning promotion, John had thought of me.

'We all thought Leroy was quite impressive because of what he had done at Torquay. It was a hard time for the club. Martin Allen had done a great job getting us into the play-offs two years running but a lot of the team had left, including the likes of DJ Campbell. We were owned by the supporters, there was no money, and we needed someone who could manage differently and on the training pitch.'

Greg Dyke, *Brentford chairman*

I went to the interview, confident and well prepared. I had experience of League 1 and, although the club had lost several senior players, I studied the squad and I felt I could work with it. I was still full of confidence after what we had achieved at Torquay, and I walked in to meet Greg Dyke and his directors knowing I could impress.

I surprise people in interviews. I always have. I enjoy walking in, and opening my mouth and seeing eyebrows visibly rise. Even when I was young, talking to teachers or coaches, and now looking for work in football. Leroy; probably uneducated, probably not eloquent, black. Then I talk, I'm prepared and I have some knowledge. Then I have their attention.

The job was mine. I knew I needed to work some transfer magic and unearth some players to add to a weak squad but the big mistake I made that day was not interviewing Greg and the club properly. I left the room, hopeful that I had some elbow room to build something but no one ever mentioned just how empty the club's coffers were.

I ran into the former manager, Martin Allen. I had once replaced him at Wembley as a sub in the League Cup Final, and here I was doing the same in perhaps a less glamorous part of the capital. We chatted and Martin said, 'There's nothing there, Leroy.' I listened but as I say, I had worked with 'nothing' at Torquay and was confident I could do the same.

The thing is, whereas whatever little money the club made at Torquay went back into the squad, at Brentford it was soon clear that such were the dire straits at the club, the squad was going to be left to fend for itself.

Good senior pros such as Sam Sodje and Michael Turner were sold for decent money but those funds disappeared to cover the club's debt. I did get Jo Kuffour back from Torquay and the likes of Adam Griffiths from Watford, but I was trying to box clever, look at free transfers and non-league football, and when several injuries kicked in, it was the youth team that had to provide cover, whether they were ready or not. When they said they wanted someone to develop players, they weren't joking.

I was annoyed. Annoyed with myself for not getting the truth from the board and annoyed with Greg for not being forthcoming with the financial facts. I really like Greg. He was passionate, amazing at his job, a great businessman but also a football man. He loved Brentford. Loved them. I just would have appreciated more transparency regarding just how troubled the club were at the time.

Tracksuit on though, I took to the training ground with as much enthusiasm as I had at my former club, but unlike Torquay, it became very clear, very quickly that this set of players weren't going to ride my wave of zealousness with the same fervour as their peers down in Devon.

The club had sold senior players, but the ones left were very much indoctrinated in Martin Allen's methods. Martin had drilled certain things into them. No disrespect to Martin at all, that's good management, but because I wanted to work a certain way and get them playing a very different way, their inability or reluctance to change meant my task was that bit harder.

Under Martin, they had been instructed when to release the ball, have a touch and get it forward. I came in and wanted them to take responsibility, I wanted them to trust each other. I wanted them to back themselves and think for themselves but I I could see from an early stage that they weren't buying into my methods. I was also promoting the young players and when you do that from sheer necessity, and then take those kids to play at big clubs such as Nottingham Forest, it is going to be hard.

I'm not trying to make excuses or plead hard luck. I had accepted the job and it was up to me to work hard and get the best from what I had. We actually started well, winning our first game at home to Blackpool, and staying unbeaten for the first six fixtures.

'I jumped at the chance of rejoining Leroy in London but it wasn't working for him. I could tell the players there weren't quite up for the changes he wanted to make. I do believe though that had he brought half the Torquay team along with me, he'd have been at Brentford for a very long time.'

Jo Kuffour, Brentford player

Luci and I had bought a place in London and it was great to be back near my family and the boys as Liam was at Fulham and

Daron was playing rugby at Rosslyn Park. We might have rented, but I was adamant that although I was only on a tenuous, one-year rolling contract, I had to commit. Treat the job with respect and give it your all. That was the only way to work. Football is all about short-termism and you get used to it (my longest contract in any form of football was four and a half years at West Ham) but I wanted to be firmly in London, in body and in mind.

Those first six games had gone well and while I could see, through time with my players on the training pitch that things would be hard, the fans and the board were pleased. In 2006, the club had become the first professional outfit to be fan-owned. It was new and exciting, and for a manager, I guess it meant even more fan scrutiny than usual.

I had brought Paul Mortimer along with me to Brentford. I hadn't had an assistant as such at Torquay, but he had helped out and Paul and I were very close friends and worked well together. He had been my apprentice at Fulham and had gone on to have a good career at several clubs. We had hit it off, becoming friends and enjoying many occasions with our wives and kids but also with Derry sitting about chatting about nothing but the game.

Paul and I worked hard every day at the training ground and often we did it publicly. The club was very supporter-orientated and our training sessions had become open to the fans. It was refreshing and I certainly didn't mind working like that. At these sessions though, fans and directors would see us working with youth players and when things started to go wrong on matchdays, they might have hoped for me to hand out more bollockings.

'I had been Leroy's boot boy at Fulham and he gave me some stick, which I gave straight back. Now that was not the done thing back then but I think Leroy liked it and we became great friends. I jumped at the chance of working with him at Brentford because I felt I could learn from him. The idea that he was too nice makes me laugh.

'At Brentford, early in the season, we took a group of fringe players who hadn't played much to Hampton and Richmond. We didn't have a reserve side, so myself and Scott Fitzgerald, the youth team coach, took this group down there. Leroy came to watch and it was clear in the first half, that these guys were rusty. We got them in at half-time, and Scott and myself had our say while Leroy stood quietly in the corner. We said this and that – all positive stuff – and then I asked if Leroy wanted to say anything.

'He stepped forward and from nowhere, he went absolutely ballistic. I mean completely crazy. I was scared. There was saliva coming out of his mouth, he was nose to nose with some of them, wide-eyed and manic like I'd never seen before. "Now fucking get out of here," he screamed and off they went, as shocked as Scott and I.

'Then he turns to us, and calmly says, "Right, quick cup of tea before the second half." A complete change. Later I had to bring it up and ask what had happened in that dressing room, and he explained that these players need to know that it might happen. It could happen. Do it once, and put it in your back pocket. Then the players will be slightly on the back foot, knowing it could come. That breeds motivation.'

Paul Mortimer, former team-mate and
assistant at Brentford

It was when these very young players came into the first team, for reasons other than their ability, that I would never just scream at them. I know when to have a go but these were kids. Not just young pros but kids, being asked to make the step up, not because they were necessarily ready to, but because we needed them to. Me screaming at them, and digging them out for getting things wrong would have vented some of everyone's frustration but it wouldn't have helped them. In fact I might have finished some careers.

I had a duty to those young men. I'm sure that those watching, both at the training ground and on matchdays, might have taken that style of management and come up with the notion that I was too nice. Frankly, that was bollocks.

The way I had worked with the players at Torquay was the way I was going to always work, had I had a longer time in club management. I wanted to develop players, help them to believe in themselves and their team-mates. Would I scream? As I say, only when necessary. Would I let players communicate with me, myself, and most importantly, each other? Damn right I would.

I recently read a newspaper article by Matthew Syed in *The Times* about innovation in the game and how football can learn from other sports. In it, Syed cited Saracens Rugby Club. There, they had created a family room at the training ground where wives, girlfriends and kids could all mingle. 'We wanted to provide an opportunity for the partners of the players to meet, to have a coffee and to chat, to feel like part of a family,' said Mark McCall, the club's head coach. 'That leads to a broadening and deepening of relationships of the players, too. This has an impact on the culture of the club, the sense of togetherness, and ultimately, upon performance.'

Not rocket science and the key word is always performance but it makes you think. They then put microphones on the players during training and they noted just how improved the level of communication had become between the players. 'They had developed greater familiarity on and off the pitch,' wrote Syed. It got me thinking about my time coaching. At Torquay I hadn't created a family room at training – we only had one hut – but I had invited communication and honesty. I had wanted the players to back themselves when communicating with me and each other, because then they would do the same on a Saturday, and they had.

At Brentford I had assessed my playing staff and given their age, ability and short time in first-team football, I was absolutely not going to hinder their development or lose their trust by screaming at them, be it in the dressing room, matchday or on the training ground in front of all the fans. Too nice? I'd like to think it was merely common sense.

It is though a results business. I know that and I'm only underlining reasons for the difficulties both myself and the club were having. Having reached the heady heights of fourth after our good start, the wheels came off. Injuries and bad form followed and for the next 18 games, we failed to win a match.

'It was hard. Martin Allen had been bloody hard to work with but the fans loved him so whoever replaced him was going to have a job winning them over. We played some ordinary football and the results matched that. This was a club owned by the fans, but the supporters turned on the fan owners! That's football. At the end of the day, supporters just want their team to win, they don't care who is running the place. The atmosphere got nasty and decisions had to be made.'

Greg Dyke

These are the hard times. Loss after loss, draw after draw, with the locals getting restless and each game taking on more importance with the pressure ramped up. You can't leave the job at the ground. You can't take off the tracksuit and just go home and smile. I couldn't, anyway. Instead I would go home and stare at the wall, the ceiling, thin air. Anywhere but at my partner, who, unknown to me, was being ignored.

'I could see Leroy's mood changing. We were getting absolutely no support from the club and had cobbled together a side, but every week we just didn't know what these young, untested players would give us. We worked on the training pitch but it was so hard. Here's a good, young manager getting no support to improve himself and the team. Leroy became very quiet, I sensed his frustration. He began to smoke cigarettes which was a clear sign of his anxious mood. We were getting beat every week and I could see the club weren't going to step forward to help. Leroy is so upbeat and he was trying to be, but there was a change in him.'

Paul Mortimer

Soon the level of abuse from the fans at Griffin Park was becoming more and more vociferous. You stand in the technical area trying to win a football match but in your mind you're thinking, the board can hear these boos and screams. The clock starts to tick until one day, you're there alone and you know, you just know, that today is the day.

That day came in November at home to Crewe, who were managed by Dario Gradi, a byword for longevity in the mad game of football management. His side battered us 4-0. Towards the end, I told Paul to stay in the dugout. I needed to stand alone and take the abuse that was now flying down from the stands and seemed to resonate from all corners of the old west London stadium.

'Two weeks before the Crewe game, the chief executive called me to the office and tried to get me to criticise Leroy. I now realise it was my interview for Leroy's job. I had a row with him as he was trying to put words in my mouth. That was never going to happen.'

Paul Mortimer

It's hard. You're human. Of course it's hard. I was used to far worse though. I had played as a black man at Leeds and Millwall in the early 1980s remember. The thing was, I understood it. I have never supported a football team like the punters screaming for my head that afternoon, but I am immersed in football and I got that this was their life. Some may scoff that it's not Barcelona but to fans who come week in and week out, it's bigger than that.

I was a symbol of the club's poor fortunes. I was presiding over a winless streak that these people were desperate to see halted. I got that and so I stood there, knowing that soon, I would be beckoned to the boardroom and this would be over. Disappointment but also relief. I went into a bubble, readying myself for the next few hours. At the forefront of my mind was the team, most of them very young, who weren't ready for this sort of occasion.

At the whistle, Dario put his arm around me and whispered, 'You'll be okay, Leroy.' He knew I was working on a shoestring, he after all had done the same on so many occasions, and so I headed into my dressing room and told my players that they had given me their all. They knew my time was up as much as I did and while this sounds like the condemned man waiting at the gallows, I kept the mood upbeat. And then I made my way to the boardroom. I wasn't in there long. Greg told me his reasons, and I nicely walked out of the door. I didn't take it personally; if you do that in football, you're fucked.

> 'It was such a shame the way it ended. It seemed Leroy was a victim of his success at Torquay because Brentford had, instead of wanting Leroy, the forward-thinking, brilliant and knowledgable coach, they had seen a guy who could work with nothing and put fires out. He's better than that and deserved better.'
>
> **Paul Mortimer**

I went back to the dressing room, said my final goodbyes and glanced out of the dressing room window. Vast numbers of fans had gathered outside, along with a big police presence and as my car was parked away from the club car park, I must admit to feeling a little apprehensive.

Time to front up though and so I left the stadium, to a roar of boos and catcalls, and with police flanking me as I made my way through the crowd, I left Griffin Park for the last time. The abuse was strong. 'Leroy, you're shit!' 'Rosenior, you're a fucking disgrace.' 'Fuck off, Rosenior.' It was like a serial killer being led from a court to the prison van, but I didn't have the benefit of a blanket over my head.

I walked through, head up, shoulders back and then a sense of respect and a feeling of progress came over me. For all the abuse I was getting, none of it, not one scream, was racial. Now, that might sound trivial to some, but it resonated with me so much that I got in to my club Ford Focus (I told you they were skint) car and felt a certain level of respect for the baying mob and relief that it was over.

> 'Brentford fans have always been quick to condemn. I left the ground that evening and the fans were still there all shouting at me, "What about you Dyke? When are you fucking off?"'
>
> *Greg Dyke*

Relief though only lasts so long. When you're sacked you drop into a mini depression so if Luci thought she might have got back her partner who is once again emotionally engaged, she was wrong. Football, and especially management in football, makes you very introspective. You are constantly thinking about *your* team, *your* tactics, *your* job. Then you get asked to leave and you're wondering what *you* did wrong and why *you* didn't make it work.

Those internal questions turned to frustration when my youth team coach, Scott Fitzgerald, took over as caretaker boss and was given funds – *FUNDS!* – to bolster the squad. It reiterated the fact that the link between directors and coaching staff while I was there was a broken one. I dwelled on it, going further into a hole, one that only a simple conversation one night with Luci could pull me from.

'Leroy, you haven't spoken to me for 18 months. Not properly.' Her words hit me hard. She was right. Since leaving Torquay, I had been in my own bubble. It had happened in my marriage when my knee took over my thoughts and now it was happening again. This time it was my managerial career that had become the mistress threatening to ruin a relationship.

That's when I started to wonder about the career path I was on. After Brentford, my phone remained silent. I would get other managerial – albeit short-lived – opportunities but when I looked at Luci that night, I realised what was at stake. Luci was pregnant with our second child and it made me think about Liam and Daron. I can't remember much about my eldest boys as children. I would take them to football, but that was the issue, everything revolved around football, to the detriment of real life.

> 'Being the son of a footballer, it can be distant. That's no slight on Dad, he's been a wonderful father but you do have to get used to life with an athlete's focus often being elsewhere. For my brother Liam it might be different because he clearly wanted to be a footballer too and also had that focus but for me, I didn't have that and then maybe it becomes harder to relate.'
>
> **Daron Rosenior, Leroy's son**

Luci and I decided to move back to Bristol. I hadn't totally dismissed the idea of management but if I did do it again, could

I go about it in a different, healthier way? Is that even possible?
My mind started to wander and to think about different options,
different career paths. Football was in my blood and I was not
going to leave it but having been stung by the Bees, perhaps it was
time to explore a different honey pot.

14

Ten-Minute Wonder

Wednesday 16 May 2007, 4.21pm

My phone rings and the name of my old chairman at Torquay, Mike Bateson, is on the screen. 'What do you want?' I ask menacingly.

'Leroy, I'm really struggling to sell the football club.'

'I'm not buying it,' I tell him.

'No, no. What I need is someone to come in and look after it for me. I trust you and I'd like you to come in and just oversee things until I get a buyer. It could be six months, it could be a fortnight. What do you say?'

Thursday 17 May 2007, 12.12pm

I meet Mike and we agree some loose terms. I won't move back down from Bristol, I'll only come in for a couple of days a week but with only six registered pros at the club, I will try and build him a football team, ready for the following season.

Saturday 19 May 2007, 2.34pm

A press conference at the Plainmoor stadium in Torquay. A reporter asks me how I feel coming back to the club I had left just over a year before. 'I'm buzzing,' I answer. 'I love this club, it's great to be back, blah, blah, blah.'

Saturday 19 May 2007, 2.44pm
With the press gone to write their stories and the press conference being shown on Sky Sports News, my phone rings. It's Mike, 'Leroy, you're not going to believe this.'

'What, Mike?'

'I've sold the club.'

Mike liked a prank. 'You're winding me up, Mike.'

'I'm not. The consortium interested saw the press conference on the television and realised, having appointed you, I was serious about keeping the club and they've agreed to the terms. I've sold it. Oh, and they want their own manager.'

Friday 25 May 2007, 9.47pm
Unemployed, I sit on the living-room sofa watching *Have I Got News For You*. Suddenly, in the Odd One Out round, my face pops up and Hislop and Merton are discussing my ten minutes as Torquay manager and that I now have the dubious honour of presiding over the shortest tenure ever in the history of football management.

Fame at last.

15

Planes, Pains and Automobiles

THE sun shines over Croydon. Buses roll down the Brighton Road, old women make their way to the shops, school kids tease each other, carrying their greasy boxes of chicken, and estate agents hurry from properties to their company cars. A normal, everyday English road. Nothing to see here.

Paul Mortimer and I are strolling back to his house from the train station, wearily pulling our luggage behind us, having endured the sort of month and journey that not many football managers could ever envisage. We turn to each other. Our tired mouths crack a smile and that smile soon becomes a chuckle and within seconds we're doubled over laughing. 'Bloody hell, Leroy,' Paul says. 'No one will ever believe that.'

* * * * *

Like so many good stories, ours started in the Orient, but in this case it was Leyton Orient. The Sierra Leone FA had contacted me to ask if I would help coach and manage their national team for one friendly fixture against the O's at Brisbane Road in the spring of 2007. Sierra Leone had a couple of African Nations qualifiers coming up and it was felt that they could assemble their players in London – many of whom played in Europe – coach them properly, organise them and, having failed to qualify for the tournament, seek to improve the squad with an eye on a better future.

I had just had my ten minutes of fame at Torquay, I wasn't working and was more than happy to help in London. I asked Paul to come along and assist me and he jumped at the chance. Paul and I enjoyed working together. Firm friends and old housemates in Bristol, we got each other. We got each other's sense of humour and we got how the other liked to work.

Paul is a football nut and a damn fine coach and as a manager I liked to work with someone I could trust to just get on with the coaching side of things. He was honest with me too. We had become such good friends that neither had a problem pulling the other one up on something and shining a light on a moment of stupidity. In football management, that is invaluable.

So we took the team, coaching them on the plush sports grounds of Dulwich College. The standard since I had played for the country, over a decade before, had risen considerably with players coming to us from their domestic league teams in England, Sweden, Italy and Belgium.

These guys could play and we merely polished their teamwork and got them organised in a way that perhaps they hadn't been before. We went to Leyton Orient and we beat them – no, smashed them – 4-1. I was impressed and, as it happened, so were the Sierra Leone FA.

You'll remember my dad's advice when I told him I was going to play for the country of his birth. 'Don't do it, son.' Well, his advice when I told him that his motherland now wanted me to manage their side was pretty much the same but I could see the pride in his eyes that I was in demand, and he understood that I wasn't going to pass up this chance.

I was never going to manage England, however much I would have liked to, so to be asked to be in charge – albeit for the remaining two fixtures of their qualifying campaign – was both exciting and fascinating to me. I've mentioned how I don't like to not work and so here I was with Paul at the airport getting ready to board a flight to Freetown for the managerial adventure of a lifetime.

I had wanted to take the team for the two games but the long-term plan was to set up regular coaching sessions in Europe, Paris preferably due to its central location. I thought I could use the two games at the end of the qualifying campaign to assess how everything looked and go from there. As it turned out, I did assess how everything worked and that's why I only lasted two games!

We arrived late at night. I brought my son Daron and my nephew Job along for the experience too. Daron hadn't been over for years and I wanted him to see his grandparents' home once again, but also to get a taste of this mad adventure I was on.

> 'I had played rugby to a good standard but loved football and wanted to work within it. I'm not sure what my role was – I think I was the team mascot – but what an experience. It certainly opened my eyes to a lot of things!'
>
> *Daron Rosenior*

The madness began right away. Usually you can get a ferry from the airport into Freetown but on this occasion, no. Instead we were presented with a helicopter. Not the flash, comfortable kind of aircraft you might see politicians or film stars arriving at events in. No, this was an old German army thing. I had never been on one before but this – in the middle of the night – did not fill me or my travelling companions with excitement.

There were no doors. It was like something out of *M.A.S.H.* You couldn't hear yourself think and I hated it. With our feet securely back on land, we got to our hotel and got a good night's sleep. No food brought to my room all night on this occasion.

The players had arrived so we drove to the city centre to the national stadium for a first training session. On arrival, while walking across the pitch, I nudged Paul. We had had about 20 players for the game in London weeks before but now were confronted with at least 35. It seemed that anyone of Sierra Leone an heritage playing football anywhere in the world had been invited. The first session was going to have to be about narrowing things down.

We started training and looking at what we had and I remember turning around and the stadium behind us was absolutely packed. People in their thousands had come to see us work and I must admit I was touched not only by the numbers but by the gratitude shown by everyone there who felt I had come to their country to help. It was like we were superstars.

> 'That was weird. I'd grown up with a famous dad, but he was never mobbed like this. This was crazy and my overriding memory of the trip was people. Lots and lots of people. Everywhere. It was also strange for me because I was the only light-skinned person anywhere. That was an eye-opening experience.'
>
> **Daron Rosenior**

All through the week, a new player would knock on our door and introduce themselves as wanting to play. They came from as far away as Vietnam, and as much as I admired their keenness to play for the side, well, too many cooks can spoil the broth.

I recall going to one new player's room, having been told we had a slight problem by the hotel manager, and being met by about 15 of his family, strewn across the floor and bed, sleeping. 'Boss,' the player said, 'no one in my family has ever been inside a hotel room.' What can you do? I wasn't going to throw anyone out so having smoothed things over with the hotel, they stayed.

The witch doctor that had accompanied the team when I played was nowhere to be seen but we did have a priest who would conduct these hour-long prayers before training. By the end of the week, knowing the longevity of his sermons, we would butt in after 20 minutes with a decisive 'Amen' to ensure we could get on with our work.

We were playing Togo, who were good. Emmanuel Adebayor was their top man and also starring for Arsenal in the Premier League. We had had to send people away which was tough because being involved in the squad meant an allowance. Cash. Denying people that livelihood meant so much here but you had to do it. Not that that cash was forthcoming. On the morning of the match, the players were going on strike due to not being paid. There were lots of raised voices and I, despairingly, went to the FA and argued the players' case. It was resolved and we could concentrate on some football.

I named the squad and gave the players their shirts and numbers. They were soon discarded and the players began to swap their shirts. 'What are you doing?' I asked. It turns out each player had a superstition about numbers and if they had their unlucky digit, well, they were swapping. Okay, carry on.

I've never been in a busier dressing room. It was huge but you couldn't move for hundreds of people. Hardly the ideal environment to work, especially as one woman was in with us, handing out match tickets through the dressing room windows to hordes of crazed fans outside. I remember Paul telling her she shouldn't be doing that, but I suggested that we just note these things down, and get on with it.

Back then, in the African Nations, when you hand in a teamsheet, passports are checked against the names to make sure the right person is playing. In the corner of the room, one of the

FA officials was making passports! Highly illegal I'm sure and I can't imagine a forger being in many national team entourages, but there you go. You could smell the glue.

It was time to play and I remember walking out on to that pitch into the most hostile atmosphere I'd ever experienced. Paul and I stared at each other and looked up at the floodlight pylons where hundreds of people had climbed to be part of the night. Army men with machine guns, a noise like you wouldn't believe. It wasn't scary but, having never seen anything like it, it was intimidating.

Daron was on the bench with me and his eyes lit up at the sheer madness of it all. Once the whistle went though, I was the manager and it was time to focus.

We'd worked on organisation. We'd worked on the basics of keeping a shape and making life hard for our superior opponents. The plan worked. We did very well, succumbing only to the one goal, and being given a rousing ovation from a crowd that had perhaps become accustomed to heavier defeats.

> 'The home crowd might have been impressed with Dad's work but they were less pleased with the referee. I can't recall what he had done in terms of his decision-making but I got the impression that by merely officiating over a defeat made him and his assistants public enemies and I remember the crowd, filling up plastic bottles with urine and throwing them on to the pitch. We were all ushered off with riot police protecting us from a soaking with their plastic shields. Madness.'
>
> **Daron Rosenior**

'That's the best we've seen' seemed to be the consensus from the less angry supporters and officials, and Paul and I took pride in what had gone on. We went back to the hotel and feeling good about ourselves, we were visited by an official who had some 'terrible news'.

The helicopter that had taken us from the airport to Freetown had crashed, killing 19 people, mainly Togolese FA delegates, including the country's sports minister. We'd sat in that thing with trepidation just days before this tragedy. I'll never go on a helicopter again.

The next game was three weeks away so we returned home, before coming back to prepare for a final match in Mali. We went back – having received half of our fee – to meet with the squad in Freetown, looking forward to meeting up and working more with the players we felt we had helped to improve. Not one of them were there.

Those players who did so well against Togo hadn't been paid and collectively had stayed away. We were greeted by local players who, no disrespect, showed us in that first session that they weren't going to be up to the job at hand. Mali were good and housed Seydou Keita, Barcelona's defensive midfielder at the time.

We had a job to do though, and having done our best, we got ready to head to Mali. We were told it was roughly an eight-hour journey. Not ideal but no problem. The thing is, of course, there was a problem. Immediately.

The team bus was packed with people, people I'd never seen before but – with the promise of an allowance if you were part of the travelling party – they had chosen to be involved. There wasn't even room for the kit so it went on people's laps and under chairs, and as for the management, well it was decided that we could drive in convoy in a tired-looking 4x4 jeep. Off we went.

We were on a long dusty road when the thing broke down, so we thumbed down the team bus and got in, sitting crammed in any nook we could find. The road had been denied the luxury of tarmac so every crater and hole was an attack on the spine and joints. My old knee wasn't thanking me for taking this job.

It took 11 hours just to get to Dakar, from where we were flying to Mali. I didn't even know that. Yes, we were naive (have a look at a map, Mali is a long way from Freetown) and now it was time to get our heads down in a hotel before the next day's flight. I say hotel, it was more like a medieval prison and with cockroaches for nightly companions, a good night's sleep was easier said than done.

We woke to the good news that the FA had got us a car and a driver so I sat in the back of an old Peugeot 504, between two officials, with Paul – who was nursing a very sore back – in the front. Off we went. It was first thing in the morning and after a couple of miles, the car made this crazy noise and it turned out that the clutch had slipped. Our driver put it back in but soon it happened again. This was repeated for the whole journey and with the airport in sight, we approached a huge roundabout at rush hour.

As you can imagine, there are no rules to roundabouts in Dakar, and as we approached it, the clutch went again. We couldn't stop so we went around this thing at about 30 miles an hour, dodging cars, Paul and I were screaming, eyes shut and awaiting an almighty bang, before somehow arriving at the back of the airport. Seemingly oblivious to our shredded nerves, the driver went to open the boot but the lock came off in his hand. Paul and I looked at each other as this guy took a screwdriver to the car boot. *This wouldn't happen to Sir Alex Ferguson!*

The back seats were eventually removed so we got our bags and we headed to the next phase of a journey that had already taken a day. We looked at each other in the airport and considered leaving, heading home and abandoning the team. Why not? This was a nightmare but there's something about football, something about being a manager of a team so we stayed, which was the right thing to do.

We landed in Mali, a beautiful country, had a a lovely hotel and headed out for something to eat but suddenly there was a monumental storm that later smashed through Paul's bedroom. He ran into mine in his boxer shorts as wind and rain screamed across his bed.

Matchday and we knew our backs would be against the wall in what was as mad an atmosphere as the one in Freetown, but having endured that journey, we hoped we could endure anything. Some of our players suggested that however well they played, the game would be lost. That was a bit worrying but what can you do?

After five minutes the referee gave Mali a penalty. I was outraged. It looked a dodgy one to me and I was up screaming at the official. He looked over, telling me to sit back down, and I rubbed my thumb and my two fingers together at him, as if to say 'you've been paid'. I was sent off.

Followed by armed guards, I took my seat up behind the directors' box and watched my team go 3-0 down by half-time. I got up to go to the dressing room where I hoped I could help prevent the haemorrhaging with some choice words, but the guard with the gun stood up with me, showed me his rifle and let me know with his eyes that I was to go nowhere.

Paul had wondered what had happened to me so he had given the half-time chat and on walking out had looked up for me, but with no joy. 'Couldn't you see me?' I asked after the game.

'No,' he replied. 'I'd looked up and realised that you were among 20,000 other black people. I'd have picked you out back home!'

We lost 6-0 which was far from ideal but after the match, Paul and I just wanted to get out of there. Cars and bikes crashed into our bus as traffic rules seemed to have – like our will to live! – gone out of the window. Paul and I had had the wherewithal to book our flights back to Europe when we landed so we picked up our luggage from the hotel, said quick goodbyes and headed for the airport. You've never seen a manager and his assistant get out of a ground after an international so fast in your life. We knew we'd never get paid but that was fine. Just show us the way to go home.

The usual African visa problems meant we paid an extra few hundred quid, but that was fine, and we were soon airborne and landing in Paris. In the French capital (or civilisation as we by now saw it) our problems were far from over. Two dishevelled, tired-looking black guys with African stamps all over their passports drew suspicious and curious responses from officious customs officers so, agonisingly close to home, we were asked to step into a side room for a little chat.

We tried hard to explain what we'd been up to for the last few days but even as I spoke, I knew the tale sounded too far-fetched, too strange, too outlandish to let us be on our way. Us two, international football managers? No chance. They weren't believing us. We would have to be searched thoroughly. And that's when we heard it. *Thwack!* The sound of a blue medical glove being put on behind us and that's when I snapped. 'What the hell do you think you're doing?' I roared. 'You have no right to lay a finger on [or in!] us. We've done nothing wrong, now let us just get home.'

Maybe it was the genuine anger and frustration in my eyes but after much more deliberation and passport checking (but no orifice examining) the authorities let us go and we boarded our plane over a beautiful looking English Channel and touched down at London City Airport.

After a train to Croydon there we were, just hours after having a storm in our hotel room and a machine gun in my face, walking down this familiar and blissfully boring English high street. And they say that the England manager's job is a thankless and intrusive task. Don't make me laugh!

16

Cracking The Glass Ceiling

IT was around 2003. I was at an event for Show Racism The Red Card, an anti-racism organisation that uses football as a tool to campaign and educate. Gordon Taylor, the chairman of the Professional Footballers' Association, was there and he came over to me, knowing that I had recently taken and passed the new Pro Licence coaching badge.

I was still at Bristol City's academy but it was known that I was looking for a managerial position in the Football League. 'Hello, Leroy,' Gordon said.

I've always got on with Gordon and we shared friendly small talk and got to talking about the Pro Licence course and what I hoped to do with my new qualification. Gordon then said something that stuck with me, 'We're all rooting for you.'

It was a simple and courteous thing to say, but I left realising that those of us from black or ethnic backgrounds trying to break into coaching had an extra responsibility. It wasn't an added pressure – all I wanted to do was work with players, make them better and see progression at whatever club I was managing – but like the players who had paved a way for me in the 1970s and early 1980s, coaches of ethnic backgrounds were being watched, assessed in a way others weren't; not only in terms of their own career but in how they could inspire future generations.

I am not working in football management for many reasons. I have made it clear that part of me felt that the total fixation and single-mindedness that a manager needs to have (even in the lower leagues) might not be healthy for me and my family. I'm not sitting here, saying I could have been a top Premier League manager had I been given more opportunities but the facts are, after my stint with Torquay, Brentford and then Sierra Leone, the phone stopped ringing.

I was never asked to even interview for another job, let alone be asked to do one and as a father of a professional footballer who himself has ambitions to break into coaching and management, I'd be lying if I didn't ask questions about where we are in this country when it comes to black and ethnic minority coaches being given a fair crack of the whip.

As I took stock after my short adventure in Africa, I wondered why the phone was so silent. When it came to my coaching I was very confident and backed myself – given time and support – to be able to do well in any position I took on. I looked from afar and saw the managerial merry-go-round spinning and the same old faces hopping on and off.

It has to be said that white managers were losing their jobs, getting paid off, doing a bit of media work and getting offered something new just months, sometimes weeks, sometimes days later. I looked at my own experience but also those of Paul Ince and John Barnes, two men with incredible playing careers behind them but having been sacked from a second job, were left looking at a telephone seemingly as quiet as mine.

To get far in football management you have to be good, of course you do. If you're not then you will get found out. Players know, fans know. If you're faking it and going through the motions, they'll know. My god, even some club directors might see through you. What I have always questioned is opportunity and the lack of it afforded to black would-be managers and coaches.

A 2016 report compiled for the Houses of Parliament by Loughborough University, the Fare Network and the Sport's People's Think Tank, revealed that only '20 out of 493 senior coaching positions at professional clubs are held by BAME [Black, Asian and Minority Ethnic] coaches: 4.1 per cent'. The fact that these figures were put together prior to Jimmy Floyd Hasselbaink losing his job at QPR in the autumn of 2016 is depressing enough before you realise that the figure, while rising from the 3.4 per cent in 2014, is down from the 4.2 per cent of 2015.

In fact, the only BAME manager appointed from the 73 positions filled in 2015 was Hasselbaink. In the Premier League only four of the 119 senior coaching positions are BAME. That's a worrying 3.4 per cent. The report concluded by saying, 'It remains disappointing to note that since the first report in 2014 the figures have changed very little; the data continues to show that if you are from a BAME background and aspire to be a manager or coach, you are at a disadvantage.'

No one is asking for jobs to be given to people solely to raise quotas and appease the likes of me. This is about opportunities. I've mentioned before that I have enjoyed surprising people throughout my professional life, and as I contemplated my next move after Brentford, it dawned on me that perhaps even that chance to raise an eyebrow or two at boardroom level was frustratingly hard to come by.

'What Leroy did at Brentford can't be labelled a failure. We had nothing, absolutely nothing to work with. Leroy was asking non-league players (not that I have anything against non-league, some great players have come from that level) to come in all too soon in their careers and do a job in a very competitive League 2. That wasn't failure, so how does someone with Leroy's CV, his knowledge, his success on a shoestring, how does he not get asked to at least interview for more work?

'In today's game, development is a buzz word. Money can be tight and clubs want someone who will develop players. That is exactly what Leroy was great at, but nothing. He's great with the media, a great communicator, he has respect, he has experience at every level of the English game. I'm sorry but, you have to ask why he isn't working, at least in the Championship.'

Paul Mortimer

I'd be lying if I said that each time I looked in the papers back then (and today), and saw the same white face filling a different job, I wasn't disheartened. Club owners and chairmen don't seem to think outside of the box when recruiting and for a young, black coach in today's game, getting seen past the usual candidates, even those less successful ones, is proving strangely difficult.

'The fact is, football management in this country is not an equal opportunities employer.'

Paul Mortimer

'It's not an equal opportunities employer but you can tell any white, English manager that and he would agree as they are not getting the jobs in the Premier League. The thing is, people seem to accept that and they speak eloquently about it and how changes should be made to help English managers. Now, if those people can accept that fact, why can't they accept that the same thing goes for black managers and coaches?

'That's frustrating but it's understandable. What I mean by that is you have to understand the perception that many in positions of power have of black people generally. That has nothing to do with football though. Look at the higher echelons of any big business in the UK and you will see very few black faces.

'Look in any press box in England and you see very few black faces and don't tell me there aren't any black journalists, there is a paper dedicated to black news, but it is within football, the most high-profile and media attentive of industries that it gets reported on. It is football's problem according to so many people. It isn't, it is society's and until that changes, football will merely shine a light on the bigger issue.'

John Barnes, former England international and
ex- Celtic and Tranmere manager

Perception is interesting. For so long, black footballers were seen as either tricky wingers or swashbuckling centre-forwards. Too lazy to get their shorts dirty, too tactically inarticulate to be put in positions on the pitch where responsibility was as necessary as ability. Today, we have black goalkeepers, we have black centre-halves. The defensive midfielder fills a role named after Claude Makelele, a Frenchman of African descent.

Black players were finally given chances to prove themselves as something more than what the game perceived them to be and so, today, it is those walls that coaches and managers need to break down once again.

But it isn't as easy as Brian Clough picking Viv Anderson at right-back. The fight against racism in the game has taken huge strides since Viv won his first England cap, but as John Barnes says, racism in society remains, both in overt and covert form. In my view steps need to be made to promote diversity. Black coaches aren't getting interviews for jobs, and that needs to change if manager's offices are to be representative of not only the national game, but the country as a whole.

> 'If you look at the English national team, from the under-16s up to the senior squad, I'd say about 45 per cent of the players are black, yet they don't work with any coaches of the same background. Now, of course the coach has to be good enough but they aren't getting the opportunity and to me that is wrong.'
>
> *Paul Mortimer*

In 2002, American football reacted to the sacking of two black head coaches who both had winning records that suggested the loss of their jobs was unfair and unjust. Civil rights lawyers got involved and with the backing and work of many high-profile individuals involved with the National Football League, the Rooney Rule (named after Dan Rooney, the owner of the Pittsburgh Steelers and chairman of the league's diversity committee) was introduced to ensure that minority coaches had to be considered for high-level coaching roles.

There has been argument and counter-argument but in general the ruling has been a success and I like the idea of a similar ruling here in England. I like it because it puts coaches in front of owners. Of course it isn't about giving black coaches at any level jobs for the sake of it, that's a crude misunderstanding of the rule. No, instead it gets black and ethnic coaches in a room with club owners and experiencing the interview process. Owners and club executives may have preconceived perceptions changed in the process while coaches are afforded the time to prove their worth.

Football and the way it recruits needs a shake-up. That's at every level from the boardroom down, but too many people don't see coaching as being for them as they just don't see a historical path mapped out. I'd like to see it implemented in the Football League for three or four years and then see where we are.

Clubs are changing. Owners are no longer the local wide boy businessman with certain political views who wants someone just like him. Football's got too big, is too global and things have to change to underline that.

> 'When the Rooney Rule was first talked about in the English press, I felt it was horribly misrepresented. Journalists simplified it, and because of that many people saw it, or see it as a rule that would force club owners to give black people jobs. It is not about that all!'
>
> *Paul Mortimer*

'Yes, there was a problem with how the Rooney Rule was perceived over here. There were a lot of accusations about tokenism. Most of that criticism came from people who don't really understand what the rule truly meant and from people who don't know what it is to be discriminated against. I get lots of abuse on the likes of Twitter. Because I'm pro the rule, people sarcastically suggest that Andy Cole should get the Manchester United job. That's stupid but it raises an argument. There clearly aren't any black coaches qualified to take any Premier League job and that has to be looked at.

'It's all about opportunity. John Barnes got a big opportunity at a big club in Celtic but when that went wrong, he had to wait until he got a job at Tranmere, a club clearly on a downward spiral if you look at where they are today. Now, I suspect that had a white manager who as a player had been of Barnes's calibre, he'd have been given more chances.

'Paul Ince is the same. Even when he did well, there were the suggestions that he was lazy. All the old stereotypes used against black players in the 1970s and 1980s resurface. It's bizarre and it's wrong.'

Oliver Holt, *journalist*

'I think the Rooney Rule is a load of bollocks. Chairmen and owners might be forced to interview black people but that's as far as it will go. They have the man in mind who they want and they will get him. Look at the black guys who have managed in the Premier League. It hasn't been about their experience. It's because of their star quality. Ruud Gullit. Jean Tigana. These guys are perceived to be stars, clever footballers. It is so much harder for a black player, perhaps of lesser star quality to get a chance. I don't think many in the future will bother. John Barnes is a hero to so many black footballers. He is seen as the best but after two cracks at management, he isn't asked again. Two chances! That prejudice won't change with a Rooney Rule.'

Andrew Cole

I've heard the frustration and suggestion that all a rule of this kind offers is tokenism and somehow patronises black coaches. I totally disagree because I have been in boardrooms and been given the chance to talk to directors and chairmen, so I know how you can change attitudes.

In the 2016 report, BAME coaches claimed a 'huge barrier' in hearing about vacancies. That suggests they are not even being considered and that must change. These guys have to get in a room, there is no point moaning from afar because young coaches will think 'what's the point?' and then a generation of coaches are lost to the game.

'There hasn't been a notable route for black coaches in this country. I understand what Andrew [Cole] is saying but in America, people did take note and attitudes changed. Eventually owners weren't going through any motions and progress was visible and real.

'I was in the States recently and went to an NFL game and what struck me was the number of women going to the game. They were in big groups, the match was a social occasion for them and their female friends to go to together. There was no abuse, just a level of equality that I'm afraid is lacking in English football. Here we have such a monocultural, white, male environment and it needs to be slightly careful because there aren't enough people from an ethnic background or women involved at all levels of the game.

'Reluctant partners in this enterprise, football is not massively forward-looking and there is a thought that people want to protect what they have got rather than opening it up. It's a closed shop and that needs to change.'

Oliver Holt

I recently read that all sports will need to have at least 30 per cent of their boards made up of women or face the threat of losing National Lottery funding and that the government would refuse to sign off and back bids for key events. The FA, with only one female member on its 12-person board, was cited as being most at risk and in a world where cash – or the threat of withholding it – can raise eyebrows, you sense the right change might follow. I hope the same goes for how coaches are recruited.

Today, Football League clubs are offered a voluntary option to make sure they interview a coach from an ethnic background but is merely having the option enough? At youth level, Football League clubs must include a black or ethnic coach in the recruitment process, but now, in my opinion further steps need to be taken.

> 'Having worked in football, it doesn't surprise me that not many black coaches have made it. People can talk and say this and that and say they will abide by a rule, but at the end of the day, that's not true. They have someone in mind, and they can interview ten coaches from an ethnic background but their man that they know will end up getting the job.
>
> 'The problem is, when you run a big organisation like the BBC, which I did, you can take the decision that you are going to change how you recruit. You then go to your various different management teams and the policy is in place.
>
> 'In football, it's a series of small businesses. Each club is independent and you really have no control over them. Yes, you can make a rule but they will eventually do what they want. At Brentford, we employed Leroy, not because he was black but because of what he had done at Torquay.'
>
> *Greg Dyke, former chairman of the Football Association*

So what next? What of the future? Will it take Chris Hughton to bring his Brighton side up and for them to then do a Leicester and win the Premier League for young black coaches to have the confidence to follow? Plenty of black players won't see it as an option but surely knowing they can get in a room to at least interview and be heard will appeal.

> 'My concern is that a rule like they have in America almost lets off racist owners. Now I have to be careful when I say racist, because a lot of these guys don't even know or think they are. We all can be racist and we can all

230

be prejudiced. If they simply interview someone because they have been told to, they will still give that position to the man they prefer. They've done what is asked of them but deep down, maybe even subconsciously, they think black coaches don't have the skill set required to be a successful manager. It's that racism and those prejudices that have to be eradicated first. That takes time but that's how things change.'

John Barnes

I now look to my son, Liam, who while he still has plenty of football to play, is very keen to break into management and coaching. When he was just six or seven, rather than drawing pictures of himself scoring the winning goal in the World Cup Final, he would draw himself on the touchline as the manager in that same final. Now, how far he goes will rightly be dictated by his ability and his ability alone. What I hope is that he gets the opportunities to show off that ability.

'I fully expected to come across my dad as a manager in the Premier League, let alone the Championship. What he did at Torquay was nothing short of a miracle, not only because of the budget or lack of one he worked with but the style they played. Of course I am biased but him being my dad has nothing to do with it when I say he's up there with the best coaches I have worked with.

'People get treated differently in football, be it their sexual preference, the colour of their skin, or whatever and some black players will suppose management is not possible. For me, I want to get to manage at international level. I have probably been spurred on by my dad's negative experiences, and I know it will take a lot of hard work.

231

'You have to have a passion, be obsessed. I've seen lazy managers. They get by and expect a budget. I've seen coaches fall asleep in team meetings. There is such a lack of good coaches in this country, that if you put in the graft, and work, it will show. I know plenty of managers who hate the game.

'There are those who want to take short cuts. But look at Chris Hughton, it took him 30 years to become a manager but everywhere he has been he has been successful. He takes the training, he is the first in and last to leave. There's a correlation between his work and his success. That's what young black coaches have to think. Put it in and demand jobs through success.

'Yes, I will probably have to be head and shoulders above other, white candidates for jobs, but that drives me on. Look at what the likes of Cyrille Regis did, look at what my dad did, look at John Barnes. These guys went into the most hostile of environments because they believed in their own ability. They were successful and they changed attitudes. I want to do that from the manager's dugout.'

Liam Rosenior

'When I was at Tranmere, the fans misunderstood me when I said I got the sack because I was black. What I meant by that is they would have of course backed me if I had won every match. Fans don't care what you are if you are winning matches. But, if you lose a similar amount of games as a white manager, it is my belief you get sacked quicker.

'I'm not saying all black managers can be as good as any white manager. What I am asking is, can we please be as bad? You see lots of bad white managers not lose their jobs and eventually if they do, quickly get another position. You see bad black managers go very quickly and not come back. That managerial merry-go-round doesn't seem to have many black faces sitting on it.

'If you look at the history of racism, there has been very slow progress. Frank Rijkaard won the Champions League with Barcelona. We didn't suddenly see an influx of black coaches. Arsene Wenger and Gerard Houllier did well and suddenly everyone was employing French coaches. Racism exists but society must fix it. FIFA have decided in their wisdom to cancel their anti-racism policies as they feel their work is done. They have ticked that box. They had players wear a few t-shirts before games or in the odd ad campaign. That's that. Nothing has changed though and there is still a long way to go. That's what worries me about a Rooney Rule over here. It might just be another FIFA t-shirt.

John Barnes

The discussion will rightly continue but we also need action. Let's see what steps Liam and his generation take. John is right, racism is society's problem but such is football's reach and ability to shine a light on global problems, I have hopes that my son's drawing he did as a young boy, will become a glorious reality.

17

I'm Ready For
My Close-Up

I'M the most famous person in the world! No, really. You are finishing a book chronicling the life of arguably the most watched face on the planet. Okay, so I may be able to walk around the streets near my home outside Bristol with the minimum of fuss, and I may only get the odd 'all right, Leroy' around Brixton, but – and apologies to Donald Trump and Simon Cowell – there aren't many faces that fill the world's living rooms more than the one on the cover of the book you are currently holding.

I haven't taken leave of my senses and it's okay, all that heading I did as a player hasn't damaged my brain. It's just that now, as a pundit and presenter for Premier League Productions, the channel that beams the English game across the world, I'm broadcasting to the biggest and most diverse audience imaginable.

I'm on five live shows a week, going out to more than 250 countries. They include India, China and most of Africa. That's billions of people and it makes you think. I can be doing my *Fan Zone* show (a kind of television phone-in for planet earth) and a game we're discussing at Goodison Park can link Texas with Taiwan. That is how big the Premier League is and I feel privileged to be part of it.

An interest in the media and how it covers the game has always been there but it took the game's wonderful luminary, Jimmy Hill, to bring it out in me. The great man had already fought and won the case for the abolishment of a player's maximum wage, he'd come up with three points for a win in league football and he'd revolutionised how football is watched on television in this country so the day that he noticed that his young centre-forward at lowly Fulham Football Club might have a talent for broadcasting hardly ranks high in the annals of the game's history, but for me it was a light bulb moment.

When I re-signed for Fulham in 1986, Jimmy and I would talk a lot, mainly about football, and through our conversations he saw something – or heard something – in me that suggested I could be in front of a microphone. He put me in touch with the right people and soon I was lucky enough to be working for the old Capital Gold radio station that covered London's football, and was sat working with and learning from the very good Jonathan Pearce, and his regular co-commentator Bobby Moore.

It was some experience, one that I enjoyed and took so much from, but I was only 22 and 23 years of age, I still had a playing career to focus on but it certainly made me think about life when I one day hung up my boots. With that experience and confidence, when that day came (prematurely as it turned out) I did plenty of work as a co-commentator for BBC Radio 5 Live.

Coaching and management ambitions were still at the forefront of my busy mind but in 2006, before I took the job at Brentford, Andrew Clement at the BBC suggested I work in the studio for the channel's African Nations coverage. Mark Bright and Marcel Desailly were sent off to Ghana to do work on the ground but I was more than happy to sit on a London sofa and chat about the continent that was so much a part of my life. I loved it. It was also Jake Humphrey's first gig and he is now with BT Sport. Jake and I got on very well and I enjoyed the experience, feeling confident and at home. It was quite a leap from radio but I loved the thrill of the cameras, even if I had to work a bit in front of a mirror, perfecting my performance. And that's what it is. You have to be yourself but you also have to perform. That's why I quickly learnt to admire Garth Crooks.

Garth may not be everyone's cup of tea. I'll admit he wasn't mine when I was just a viewer but once I started to do more and more television I appreciated his (sometimes over-the-top) methods. I thought all that was a put-on, but that is Garth being Garth while also accentuating his actions. The famous nod of his, the questions that are often more interesting than the answers they seek, they are brilliant traits that Garth has developed to make a niche for himself.

Sit and be timid on a football show and the world will pass you by. Garth arrived on the scene and was talked about, not always positively of course, but he was talked about and that is why he remains such a big part of the game's television coverage today. He is known as The Chief because he can hold court within a room and for me, he was a huge inspiration. Another huge help in those early days covering the African game was the massive book given to all pundits on the show, called 'The Bible'.

This was a huge folder that covered all the teams, all the players and all the managers involved in the tournament and in those early days you would find my nose buried in it. As time went by (and I did the following tournament two years later) I was more and more confident. I had played and managed in Africa, I knew the continent well and I understood how the place worked, both positively and negatively. I could bring that knowledge to the viewer and because I did my homework, I hoped I was bringing it with some gravitas.

That necessity to be prepared was often born from sheer fear. If you are sitting in the studio, about to go on air and it suddenly dawns on you that you might not be aware of all the facts, that is terrifying. I hear pundits and co-commentators refer to players as 'the number eight' and you know that they haven't done their research. That can be fine and many good ones pull it off by sheer weight of personality but so many get stuck because they simply aren't prepared. Live television is wonderfully pulsating but it can be the most scary thing in the world if things go blank.

Fortunately my blanks were kept to a minimum and in 2009 when the BBC won the rights to show Football League coverage, I was asked to join the team for its late Saturday night slot. If they had told me how hard we would have to work on that show over the next few years I might have made my excuses and left but instead I dived right in, and thank god I did.

> 'I recall the meeting when I and the production team talked about possible pundits and Leroy's name came up. Now, because I had done some work with him covering the African Nations, my first thought, and I might have said it out loud, was, "What, the former Sierra Leone manager?"'
>
> **Manish Bhasin, *presenter of***
> **The Football League Show**

I've always been positive and having been sacked from Brentford, and having worked briefly in Africa I was able to bring something to the BBC. As a player and manager I'd worked long and hard in the Football League and knew it and its many machinations so I dived in, head first.

To be on BBC One, albeit late on a Saturday night, was a big deal. Manish and I had worked together before and there was – and is – a good chemistry between us. The fact that he is from an Asian background and I am black was also interesting and once again I have to cite Garth Crooks's role in inspiring so many like me to break into the mainstream media. Garth probably doesn't know just how his presence on our television screens allowed other black footballers finishing their playing careers to think about a career in front of the camera. Just as he had been one of the trailblazers playing the game in the early 1980s, Garth allowed black guys like me to strive for television work and he should be thanked.

Black footballers were often thought of as lazy but even the biggest bigot around wouldn't have labelled myself and Manish that if they saw the amount of sheer bloody hard work that went into doing *The Football League Show*. Filmed live (for the first few seasons until BBC cuts meant more and more of it was recorded), the show covered 72 teams over three divisions.

Our job was to cover each game, giving nuggets of information about each one, each team, player and/or goalscorer. That's significant research on a lot of teams, a lot of players and 72 managers. Use old information and it sounds stale. It was key to the show that we were up on things. This wasn't *Match of the Day*. It was on after, for perhaps the more die-hard fan. Yes, it was a slot where it was perhaps easier to fall asleep on the sofa but if we made big mistakes or were lazy with our words, viewers would know and you'd look a fool.

'Leroy brought a knowledge of the game in the lower leagues. He was so diligent, a real hard worker and that was key. You have to put things into context. For example, why a draw for one team is so special. That means a knowledge about a club's budget, injury problems, etc. Leroy knew to look all these things up. He brought all that to the table with a passion for the lower leagues. As a presenter, I loved him for that.'

Manish Bhasin

Manish and I worked. Throw Steve Claridge in too and it was such a fun team to be part of. Steve plays the grumpy card. He can come across as negative but he isn't. He knows so much about the game and like me had a real passion for the Football League but he and I are quite different in style.

I did leave it for him to take the flak from the great British public though. Steve is forthright and if he says something negative about someone or a club, it is what it is. It comes across as negative. Back then, I had a way of making even a negative comment have a positive spin. Steve would come into the office moaning that he was getting stick from fans because he said this or that. 'All I did was tell the truth,' he'd moan. He was right.

> 'Steve and Leroy could rub each other up the wrong way but only in as much as they – like so many ex-pros – long for that dressing room friction. They were chalk and cheese. Claridge would walk in wearing tracksuit bottoms, moaning about this or that that he had seen at a ground that day and Leroy would then moonwalk in, singing a song, cracking a joke. They were both brilliant to work with.'
>
> **Manish Bhasin**

It was while doing my first appearance on *The Football League Show* that my life, and my family's, turned upside down. My father had got food poisoning but complications and a serious infection saw him taken to hospital. He wouldn't come home.

For so long, Dad had been our world. Our wonderful mum was of course also everything to us all, but the Roseniors of Brixton were very much a patriarchal set-up. Not because he ruled the roost with a firm hand, no, it was his effervescence that rubbed off on everyone, wherever they were from.

Everyone who came in contact with my father was blessed by his ability as a raconteur and his knack for both positivity and humour. So it was no surprise that, when he was taken to the hospital, he said to my concerned mum, 'It's not as if I'm going to die is it?' Typical Dad.

In hospital we all sat around his bed, reminiscing about this great man, now in a coma, no longer able to say the words that brought us smiles, but whose life and very presence filled the room with memories, even as his life ebbed away. With Dad in a coma, I actually left the hospital to do that first stint on *The Football League Show* on the Saturday night. It was a huge decision for me. Should I leave? What's work got to do with anything when my own father is lying there?

The overriding voice though came from the man who meant most. My dad's. I knew he would have wanted me to go to work. 'I don't know how you did that,' one sister said to me when I came back but it was eventually understood that it was just something I had to do, for me and him, and for them. The following day he left us and while the tears flowed, within ten minutes my father's wife, his kids and his grandkids were all sitting around him, laughing about the joy he had brought us. Is there any better way to go?

The funeral was standing room only. Hundreds and hundreds of people came to pay their respects and the occasion was typical of the man. I've mentioned how dad loved a dodgy car and the series of pretty but cheap motors that packed up on him and us when we were kids.

On the day of his farewell, my car broke down on the way to my mum's house. Thanks to the AA I got there fine, but then when we left for the cemetery, with Dad leading the way, one of the limousines broke down. We were all in hysterics. God knows what the undertakers made of this crazy family laughing at what on the surface was a bit of a problem on supposedly this most sombre of days. Dad and his ability to laugh in the face of adversity was with us, for sure!

I stood and delivered Dad's eulogy and marvelled not only at the numbers present, but the smiles and the laughter that accompanied my words that day and as we walked to the cemetery with a trumpeter playing 'Oh When the Saints Go Marching In', I was the proudest any son could be.

Dad's death left a hole that will never be filled but life went on for us all and for me, a career in television blossomed. *The Football League Show* became almost cult viewing for those wanting more than just Gary Lineker, Alan Hansen and Premier League action on *Match of the Day*. We also did a midweek *League Cup Show* on the BBC and as the Football League stuff was produced by management group IMG, which also owned the rights to the Premier League, I was also working on the global channel that I am on today.

It was only when the BBC lost the rights to the Football League that I think the public realised what a good job we had all done with that coverage. I was sad to leave and look back fondly on those days, or should I say very late nights. Manish is a great presenter because he is such a big fan of the game. He asks questions, the right questions. He doesn't try to answer them, because why have pundits if the man or woman presenting knows more than them?

> 'I smile when I look back on those days doing the Football League but what I will say about Leroy is he can move. We had a night out in town when the show finished and one of my hazy memories of the night is owning the dance floor with him. The club was playing classics and there was Leroy and myself showing off our moves. Claridge was nowhere to be seen!'
>
> *Manish Bhasin*

Today, I love everything about broadcasting and I feel very comfortable doing it. Like my playing career, I get that I won't be asked to work with the biggest names such as Sky but I also hope that like my playing days, people in the know appreciate me and my work ethic. As well as the stuff I do to camera, I am also busy behind the scenes, and you'll often find me in a darkened room, trawling through hours of footage, picking out clips and talking points for other pundits to chat about. Sitting there, doing that, my Pro Licence badges come in very handy, and in the future I can see myself doing more work behind the camera.

Television is so massive today. It mustn't rest on its laurels because as good as the product is, the minute the game believes its own hype, viewers will switch off. When I played, match-going fans could rightly argue that they paid our wages. That is simply not the case anymore. Television pays the wages but what everyone involved must keep in their minds is that without the crowd in the stadium, there is no spectacle.

As I say though, the Premier League reaches all four corners of the globe and viewers, be they at home or abroad, demand good coverage. Punditry divides opinion but I am a big fan of Gary Neville. Not only does he obviously have a great knowledge about the game, he delivers his opinions in a simple way. The key is not to get overly technical, just for the sake of it. Alan Hansen was another one who changed the role of a pundit, making it more and more relevant. Myself, I don't take myself too seriously and enjoy joking with my presenters and fellow pundits and I hope our viewers relate to that.

As much as I like a joke, it is also important that you tell the truth. Football can be a masonic-like institution where people are afraid of upsetting others. I say it as I see it. Arsene Wenger, Jose Mourinho, a former team-mate, no matter – you must say what you see without fear of recrimination. Not that Jose or Arsene have my phone number anyway!

One thing I choose not to do is Twitter or any other social media. I totally understand why some like it and why some use it but my argument is that if you are on TV or the radio, and you have something interesting to say, why waste it (even if it is only 140 characters)?

Any pundit will tell you that the thrill of live telly, while never replacing the thrill of a referee's whistle, is one to cherish but it can be scary. I am lucky though because once I started to work with Show Racism The Red Card, I was going into school classrooms and trying to engage with 30 school children. Now that is nerve wracking and once I mastered that, live television was frankly a doddle.

It was while I was at Brentford that the chair of the organisation, Ged Grebby, approached me to get involved. He had heard me talk about race issues and explained that they were using football as a tool to educate. I was immediately drawn to him and what he and his team were trying to do and having given a well-received 45-minute speech at the UNISON conference (that was in front of 3,000 people and I don't care how many fans I played football in front of, that was terrifying) I agreed to do more, as long though as it was out on the road. I wanted to get in on the ground, to get into schools and talk to kids.

That is such a thrill. Getting through to kids is so rewarding. Take one school I went to in south Wales. Now the kids there, they wouldn't have seen many black people, let alone talked to them. I walked in and I guess because of the colour of my skin, I had their attention. It was harder to keep it though.

For nearly two hours we spoke about my own experiences playing football, and about cultures and what they defined racism as. Culture was an interesting one. Blank faces filled the room when I brought it up but then I asked them where hamburgers come from. They answered America. I asked where hot dogs come from. They said America or maybe Australia. I explained that Hamburg and Frankfurt are towns in Germany, hence the hamburger and frankfurter. I explained that chocolate comes from the Aztecs in Mexico. I wanted them to see that different cultures are all around them, filling even their local supermarkets. Throw in me doing some (bad) African dancing and the kids were engaged. It was so heartening to go back to the same school months later and see anti-racism posters all over the walls.

It can be frustrating that many people presume I work for the Kick It Out campaign. I respect what Kick It Out does, and I was a trustee, but for me it was key to do more away from football, and that is why I was so drawn to Show Racism The Red Card. There is only so much Kick It Out can do. So much seemed to be about talking, meeting after meeting about what could be done and while they do a lot of worthy stuff, there is a line that needs to be toed when it comes to the PFA and the FA. Of course it is great to see players speaking out on issues and wearing the t-shirts, but I wanted to be involved with doing more, especially with kids. Racism is generational and through education, it can be eradicated.

A couple of years after my dad died, I was attending the funeral of Derry Quigley, the man I considered very much as my footballing father. Derry had seen me play for London schoolboys, approached me, asked me to sign for Fulham and then had always been there as an ear and a shoulder, his dulcet Irish twang a constantly reassuring sound, even when football threatened to be too overwhelming for me to cope with.

Like my own dad's funeral, the occasion was befitting of the great man and the stand-out memory of the day was the amount of black footballers that attended. Tony Finnegan, Paul Mortimer, Paul Parker, Dennis Bailey, Kenny Achampong and many others were there, and afterwards we all had a beer and reminisced about Derry and what he had done for each and every one of us.

'When I was a boy, Derry would come over for Sunday lunch. Paul Mortimer and his young kids would come too and after lunch, with the Sunday match about to start on the telly, the kids would be allowed to run into the garden and play. Not me. I would pretend to be asleep so I could lie on the sofa, just to listen to Dad, Paul and Derry talk about the game they were watching. The way they dissected the action and discussed tactics. It was fascinating.'

Liam Rosenior

The thing about Derry was, when you were a young pro trying to make it in the game, he made you feel like you were everything. You were the only player in his life, you were the best. That gave you the confidence to carry on and persevere in a world that was frankly so tough, that many good players dropped out. At his funeral, we all realised that actually there were so many of us who had been helped by this quiet, smart Irishman, who lived and breathed football and had all our best interests at heart.

* * * * *

Today, I am a busy and happy man. I have a wonderful partner in Luci whom I love very much, five gorgeous children of whom two, Liam and Daron, have grown up into mature and brilliant young men, while Millie, Ethan and Max are younger and fill me with equal pride. My mum and sisters are everything to me and I cherish the times we are all together. I have a slight limp to remind me of a hard playing career but even that is a source of pride. The wounds of battle if you like.

My football career wasn't the most glorious or trophy-laden but it fills me with immense pride. Who knows what might have been had that knee injury not occurred just as I had made a regular habit of scoring goals in the top flight but I certainly don't dwell on it. Growing up in Brixton, I had dreamt of being a pro. I wasn't obsessed and I wasn't even the best player in my local kids' team, but I worked. I worked and I listened and I worked some more and in the end I can say that those dreams were realised.

For now, I love my work in television but ask me what I'd love to be doing in ten years and it would be working back in football management, as some sort of director of football or consultant to Liam. Add to that my other son Daron, who is a great football analyst and is currently working for Oxford United, and we might just have the ultimate footballing family business. The Roseniors. Just like my mum and dad, travelling from Sierra Leone to England in the mid-1950s, it's good to have a dream.

Epilogue

I MAY not have blue eyes, but like Frank Sinatra I have a
few regrets, one of which deserves a mention. Towards the
end of my time at West Ham, Justin Fashanu came to us on
loan. Rumours about his sexuality were beginning to take root
within the game and you sensed – even in the supposedly more
enlightened 1990s – that there were some who were uncomfortable
with his presence at the club.

One day, I was sitting in the old plunge bath with a couple
of the other lads when Justin walked into the room, dropped
his towel and joined us in the murky water. Without hesitation,
my two team-mates stood up and left the bath and the room. I
believed I knew why. I sat there in awkward silence before making
small talk with Justin, who was visibly shaken by the actions of
his fellow professional footballers.

It was a moment that changed me. For so long, I had had to
put up with a lot in order to play football. *Keep your powder dry
son*. I sat there with Justin, a team-mate, a fellow footballer, a
fellow human being and I said nothing. I didn't shout to my team-
mates, I didn't berate them for their actions, I didn't ridicule their
stupidity. I sat and I made small talk. I may as well have got out of
the bath with the others.

Justin left West Ham shortly after that and I didn't hear from
or see him again until one day while watching the news, I saw the

story that he had hung himself. My silence came back to me. Why hadn't I engaged my two team-mates, even using banter? Justin, after all, was an incredible athlete and specimen. Standing 6ft 4in, built like a racehorse; why hadn't I shouted as they left that he wouldn't fancy them anyway? They might have understood that sort of language and maybe Justin wouldn't have felt so alone. I appreciate that there were lots of other factors that drove this one-time supremely talented footballer to take his own life, but my small part in his life and in that incident saddens me.

Keeping your powder dry is all well and good but my dad would have known that there comes a time in your life when you can't let opportunities pass you by. Football had, in a way, introduced me to serious racism, but it was through football that I had got myself into a position to facilitate real change.

As a young striker, abused by opponents I was afraid, too unprepared to fuss or make my grievances clear. Almost a decade later, as I got out of that bath to get dressed, I could only imagine what was going through Justin's mind, and I realised the responsibility I had to speak out.

Writing a book gives me a mouthpiece to do just that but I hope it hasn't been read as a bitter account of my life. It is meant more of a social commentary about issues that affected plenty of other individuals, many of them not footballers, who were not in the public eye.

In the prologue of this book, I recounted the incident when I was racially abused. I haven't named the names of those involved because I feel strongly that their words came from ignorance rather than real racism. I may be wrong, only they will know, but I do believe that their nasty words toward me stemmed from the ignorant attitudes of the time and a misplaced idea that they could say anything in order to win a football match. Therefore I have merely tried to shine a light on what so many black people went through back then, and often still do today.

Twenty-five years later, I ran into one of the men who had abused me that night and I could see immediately he was regretful for his actions. He had remembered what had happened and straight away, he brought it up. That, for me, was enough. If he had been a racist I think he would have ignored it or simply forgot. Instead there was remorse and we've moved on. We're not bosom buddies, but there is no ill feeling.

'When I was at Bristol City in the youth team, we played a game in which my opponent wouldn't stop abusing me, wouldn't stop with his racial slurs. I can't say I thought about my grandad and how he had coped with it using humour or my dad who had learnt to stay calm. No, all I thought about was shutting this guy up and, having constantly asked the ref to do something about this audible abuse, my temper snapped. I chased him down, waited for him to clear the ball and whack, I flew into him and hit him hard and late. I was off. Was it the right thing to do, I'm not sure but it felt good and I guess proved that us Rosenior men can deal with racism in many different ways.'

Liam Rosenior

When my dad died, I wanted to chronicle his and my own life for my kids, for Luci who never knew me as a footballer, and for my mum and sisters. Coming from a West African heritage, playing football to a high level, managing, even appearing briefly on *Have I Got News For You*, and now working in television; some say my life has been an interesting one. I'm not sure about that and I look forward to plenty more adventures, but as a parent to both adults and children, I do look at where we are today and what sort of world their own stories will take place in.

I wanted to write that the era in which I was abused for the colour of my skin is very different to that in which we live today.

Yes, there has been massive progress but to think that similar things couldn't happen on our streets or in our football stadiums today would be both naive and wrong. Look at Brexit. Not everyone who voted for Brexit is a racist but every racist would likely have voted for Brexit and my problem with the campaign was that the rhetoric was very much anti-immigration.

I can only think about the days that my mum and dad came over to England from Africa, and had people crossing the road to avoid being near them, or those signs in windows suggesting blacks, the Irish and dogs should stay out. Today, we've seen a worrying upsurge in the same sort of nasty backlashes against eastern Europeans, especially Polish communities whose churches have been vandalised, while their people live in very real fear of physical harm.

Muslim communities of course face the same daily problems and while there is a conversation to be had about people's insecurities and concerns, my work with Show Racism The Red Card has underlined to me that it is only through open communication that people can begin to understand what is too often perceived as *other*. Only then can myths be busted. It may sound all very romantic and idealistic but that has to be better than the continual nasty trajectory we find ourselves on today.

This decade, English football of course has had to look closely at itself in the mirror. Luis Suarez's ugly clash with Patrice Evra and John Terry's presence in a court of law were proof that the game is far from (excuse the pun) whiter than white. Again, I have no idea if either Suarez or Terry are racists, but they both offered opportunities for change and what frustrated me was that Terry, then the England captain, had the chance to hold his hands up, say that he was wrong and have an honest debate about where we are and what needs to be done.

In 2014, I actually found myself involved in one high-profile incident when the former Cardiff City manager Malky Mackay was found to have shared abusive text messages with Iain Moody, his head of recruitment at the Welsh club.

Luci and I had been on holiday with the kids and were driving home. It had been a blissful August break staying in a house with no phone signal. Once on the motorway home, my mobile started buzzing frantically with a backlog of texts and voicemails and there was a common theme from media outlets. Could they talk to me about Malky Mackay? It wasn't until we were back at the house and Luci showed me an article online that I realised that Mackay and Moody were being investigated by the FA over 'sexist, racist and homophobic' text messages exchanged during their time at Cardiff.

It was a messy affair. Moody's home had been raided by police as part of an investigation into controversial transfers. Amid all the investigations, damning messages between Moody and Mackay came to light and they weren't pretty.

In July 2012, with Cardiff set to sign South Korean international Kim Bo-Kyung, an exchange between the two included Mackay writing 'Fkn chinkys'. The agent Phil Smith was referred to in another text that read, 'Nothing like a Jew that sees money slipping between his fingers.' An official at another club was referred to as a 'gay snake'. It was suggested that a French agent change the name of his firm to 'The All-Blacks' while further racist, sexist and homophobic remarks had me feeling not anger or shock (this is football – I've heard it all before), but deep disappointment. This isn't an old-school manager, this isn't a dinosaur of the past, a relic from a different time. This is Malky Mackay, a promising young coach, supposedly forward-thinking and on the verge of a Premier League job at Crystal Palace at the time.

I had been involved in the purchase of Bo-Kyung in as much as I'd been part of the Football Association of Wales's panel that decided whether he should get his work permit or not. You are sent DVDs of a player in action and study their international record and offer an assessment on what they will bring to the British game. I drove over the Severn Bridge and recall just how enthusiastic Malky was about capturing this international footballer. Again, I was disappointed to read the words that he used in private.

And that was the crux. The words were apparently in private. That was the explanation as part of Mackay and Moody's defence and the reason that ultimately saw them face no charges. Having read the initial allegations, I received an email from the League Managers' Association and in horror read their statement, that while thinly condemning the language used, argued that Mackay had been 'under great pressure', and that he was merely 'letting off steam to a friend during some friendly text message banter'.

There was that word again. Banter. That word that followed me around my career, supposedly so important to team morale, but too often letting people off for their wrongdoings. The LMA were basically saying that it is okay to send highly offensive messages because an individual is under pressure and also because that's what guys do.

When Donald Trump was revealed during the 2016 American presidential election campaign to have said the things he liked to, or couldn't help doing to women, it was brushed off as locker-room talk, something embarrassing but what guys say when they are alone together. Football's fossil-like argument that offensive behaviour is just *friendly* banter is starting to wear thin and as I read the LMA's words, my blood began to boil.

I checked my phone messages. A guy from BBC Wales had left a message, wanting an interview about the unfolding incident and I rang him straight back. 'Whoever wrote that [LMA] statement is an ignoramus,' I told him. 'Do the LMA forget who they are representing? I might be among a minority of people in the association, but I'm a member. If the LMA are going back to the Dark Ages to support people then I might have to withdraw my support.

'In the thousands of text messages I've sent I've never used inappropriate language and I'm sure neither have the vast majority of people. If Malky did send a couple of texts, as he admits to in the statement, then I'm a bit disappointed and I think it needs to be dealt with, not just swept over as a bit of banter.'

Stan Collymore tweeted, 'Disgraceful. Institutional acceptance of the "banter" of casual racism.' Football journalist Henry Winter wrote, 'The LMA looks like bumbling dinosaurs. The statement is a missive that should be filled beneath contempt.'

As the days passed I dwelt on the incident. The LMA were wrong. Their gut instinct was to protect their member in the wrong, but that means ignoring their other members and frankly, the good of the game. Football's governing bodies, if they are serious about helping to eradicate racism, need to act quickly when these incidents arise, and think of the bigger picture. Organisations like the LMA need to be proactive in educating people and I hope the incident just two years ago has gone some way in making them realise that.

I was sad that Malky missed the chance of getting the Palace job but it was a good wake-up call to those who argue that the problem is one set in our past. When Ron Atkinson was caught making racist remarks on television, his defenders argued that he had picked black players in the 1970s and therefore he could not be racist. That's like saying, 'I have a black cleaner cleaning my house.' It means nothing if the underlying attitude towards people of colour is negative and discriminatory.

I wasn't impressed that eventually the FA took no further action against Moody and Mackay but I was impressed that Mackay eventually apologised for what had happened and I believe he was sincere. Equal opportunities should be a major part of a young manager's training. Only then can the negatives of discrimination become clear. It is managers who deal with young players day to day and it is them who can help create an all-inclusive environment at clubs and within the game in general.

Recently, a poll suggested that seven per cent of football fans would stop coming to matches if a player at their club came out as gay. Now, I'd be happy to see the back of that fairly large amount of morons, but that worryingly high figure is damning. If I was a gay footballer I wouldn't come out because I don't believe the game has done enough to make that brave step any easier to take.

I'm into my 50s now, no longer a young, black footballer with something to prove but still an ageing black man seeking change. I'm confident it will come. My son Liam, like all my kids, is of mixed heritage (I personally don't agree with the term mixed race and chat with many school children who so often decide that the only race is the human race and therefore labelling anyone as mixed race suggests one parent is an alien!) as are so many, both in and out of the game.

Look around. It is so hard to label people, so difficult to pin people down by a mere glance. If you are going to judge people negatively or positively, you have to go deep, hear their words, listen to their views. That has to be good for the human race.

I'm confident that Liam, when he takes his first steps into the murky and tempestuous waters of football management, has the ability and drive to do well, but I am equally as confident that he will be judged purely on that ability and drive.

As for me, I sometimes think about my young self, standing in that shower alone, fighting back tears, confused about the game I loved and wondering if maybe the two of us weren't actually meant to be. We had our ups and downs but I'm so pleased I persevered.